Outside the Sa

Outside the Safe Place

An oral history of the early years
of the Iona Community

Anne Muir

WILD GOOSE PUBLICATIONS

First published 2011

Wild Goose Publications
4th Floor, Savoy House, 140 Sauchiehall Street, Glasgow G2 3DH, UK
www.ionabooks.com
Wild Goose Publications is the publishing division of the Iona Community.
Scottish Charity No. SC003794. Limited Company Reg. No. SC096243.

ISBN 978-1-84952-079-9

Cover photo: Reverend Raymond Bailey labouring for the masons, Iona Abbey
1939 (Raymond Bailey archive)

The publishers gratefully acknowledge the support of the Drummond Trust,
3 Pitt Terrace, Stirling FK8 2EY in producing this book.

A catalogue record for this book is available from the British Library.

Overseas distribution:
Australia: Willow Connection Pty Ltd, Unit 4A, 3-9 Kenneth Road,
Manly Vale, NSW 2093
New Zealand: Pleroma, Higginson Street, Otane 4170, Central Hawkes Bay
Canada: Novalis/Bayard Publishing & Distribution, 10 Lower Spadina Ave.,
Suite 400, Toronto, Ontario M5V 2Z2

Printed by Bell & Bain, Thornliebank, Glasgow

MIX
Paper from
responsible sources
FSC® C007785

heritage
lottery fund
LOTTERY FUNDED

CONTENTS

PREFACE

'A bunch of stories'

Shortly after embarking on the series of interviews on which this book is based, I faced a challenging question-time at a meeting of Iona Community members in London. One questioner was particularly dismissive of the concept of oral history: 'It'll just be a bunch of stories, won't it?'

He was partly right. This book *is* a bunch of stories. But to dismiss them as '*just* stories' is, I believe, a great mistake.

In the event, far from downgrading the value of stories, the collecting of this history has powerfully reinforced for me the need to acknowledge that 'stories' are all we have.

In an often-quoted verse from 1 Corinthians 13, the Apostle Paul contrasts what we can know and understand in this world of time and space, with what we shall know and understand in the next world:

'Now we see through a glass darkly, but then face to face'.

But the root of the Greek – *en ainigmati* – which is so often translated as 'darkly', translates literally as 'stories'. 'Now', says Paul, 'we see the world and the human condition reflected in metaphors – in stories.'

Some stories, of course, become more dominant over time, and they are the ones that get written up as the official histories. A book like this allows us to hear also the 'lost' stories and the 'hidden' stories which, in this context, are the stories of the islanders of Iona, the wives of early members of the Iona Community, their children, and the Community's employees.

In the end, eighty-six women and men welcomed me into their homes, and allowed me to hear their stories. I found them to be people of keen intelligence and passionate concern. Many of them had encountered great difficulty – some had faced great danger – as they tried to live out their 'Iona' insights in the world. And, despite the fact that a large number of them were, by then, in their 70s or 80s, they were still open to new ideas and fresh visions. They were, quite simply, the most life-affirming people I have ever met, and I am grateful to each and every one of them.

Anne Muir

Early days

The origins of the vision

Today, the Iona Community is known and respected worldwide as an ecumenical Christian community working for peace and social justice, the rebuilding of community, and the renewal of worship. But its beginnings were far from auspicious.

It came into being in 1938, and was virtually strangled at birth by the outbreak of the Second World War. Ironically, its founder, George MacLeod, could trace the origins of his vision for the Community back to his experiences in the First World War. Although, as his daughter Mary reveals, he rarely spoke about those times:

> 'Like many people who were in the First War, he just didn't speak about it. We do not know what went on in the trenches. But he did see inequality, and I think that's what drove him – inequality. What makes somebody want to stamp out inequality? I don't know. But certainly that was in his gut.'
> – *Mary MacLeod*

And Mary argues that the forum in which her father would fight inequality was quite consciously chosen:

> 'He was going to do law before he went to the war, but when he came back, he became a minister.'
> – *Mary MacLeod*

The effects of the inequality that George MacLeod had seen at close quarters for the first time during the First World War were even more evident in the Scotland of the 1920s. As a minister in Edinburgh, he expressed what many Christians felt:

> 'George MacLeod was very much aware of the terrible gulf fixed between the comfortably off and those poor souls who were living on pittances, due to the Means Test.[1] The contrast of these two situations was such that many Christians were very uncomfortable, but they needed someone to speak for them. George MacLeod spoke for the conscience of any sensitive Christian, and he was able, by his

own leadership, to influence people's thinking to a very considerable degree.'
– *John Sim*

One of the ways in which George MacLeod was able to influence people's
thinking was through his radio broadcasts. John Sim, later a member of
the Community, remembers hearing him, while still a schoolboy:

'We listened to George MacLeod on our battery radio, and one knew
that one was listening to awarenesses that one hadn't heard before; to
emphases which were vitally needing to be expressed in the modern
generation.

But he was not only satisfied with having said his piece. He knew
perfectly well that he had to do more than that. And so he was willing
to go to Govan to take on what was still a very large congregation, but
in a parish situation which was dire, due to unemployment. It was
there that his Christianity became extremely active in the social sense.'
– *John Sim*

As John Sim implies, George MacLeod's experience of parish ministry in
Govan was formative. Govan was an important shipbuilding area on the
south bank of the River Clyde, but during the Depression half of its
population was out of work. Annie Price was just 13 when MacLeod
became minister of Govan Old in 1930:

'Things were very bad in Govan at that time. The men walked the street
idle, and the homes were really kept going by the girls who worked in
the Co-operative factory down at the dry docks at Shieldhall.'
– *Annie Price*

George MacLeod could see that, for the vast majority of ordinary people,
the Church – his chosen agency of social change – was an irrelevance.
Douglas Trotter, one of the Iona Community's earliest members, observed
the effect on MacLeod:

'This is what hit him in Govan – how little the Church spoke to the
ordinary lives of people, certainly to the working class. He was in the

middle of the shipyards where life was pretty rough. Govan parish was only about a square mile, but teeming with folk. And George was on the doorstep, known to them all, and terribly aware of how little the Church touched their lives and meant to them.'
– *Douglas Trotter*

David Jarvie, who at that time was a member of the Young Communist League, also believes that this is where MacLeod's vision for the Iona Community really began to take shape:

'He had a packed church at Govan, but when he looked at them, there was none of the people of Govan in his church. The people were coming from all over Scotland, attracted to the charisma of George. These were middle-class people. And I think, maybe, that is where the Community grew out of. Because he realised that here he had a successful church, but the people he came to serve weren't there. The people of the shipyards weren't there. They were outside.'
– *David Jarvie*

Whether there was one moment of epiphany for MacLeod, it is hard to say, but Ian Fraser, who was associated with the Iona Community from the start, tells this story:

'George told me once that he had visited a chap in hospital who had died of malnutrition. It was found that there was only something like grass in his stomach. He had the minimum amount coming from the "burroo",[2] and he had given two-thirds of it to the family, so he didn't have enough to eat himself. That must have been very decisive for George. You're a great preacher, you've got everything before you, you've got all the adulation, you have people entranced by you, but here's a bloke who gave away two-thirds of an absolute pittance, and died of malnutrition. That's what you'd to face.'
– *Ian Fraser*

It was a stark truth: a successful church was not necessarily a relevant church. Charismatic preaching did not actually change the lot of the poor. Clearly, MacLeod would have to discover a new way of being Church, if he was going to serve the people of Govan.

Uist Macdonald was one of his young Assistant Ministers in the 1930s:

> 'There were a certain number of ministers who preached, and cele-
> brated the sacraments, but didn't realise that you must get to know
> people, see where the needs are, and help. I was lucky. I was sent to
> Govan. It was real tough stuff. We lived in the top flat of the Pearce
> Institute[3] in Govan Road, and the rest of the building was taken up
> with all sorts of things, mainly for unemployed people, to help them
> to have a place where they could go and get shelter. So we were there
> and sharing in it.'
> – *Uist Macdonald*

This is the key to understanding MacLeod's ministry in Govan: he and his
assistants 'were there and sharing in' the lives of the people. They were
living in community with them:

> 'The top flat's occupants were available to help at any hour of the day
> or night where there was need. At night, once, I was called to a house
> where a man had committed suicide, and his wife was desperate. She
> had a small shop, and couldn't face going down to it. So George went
> down to serve the early morning customers with milk and rolls, until
> help could be got. If you do things like that, what are you needing to
> do preaching for?'
> – *Uist Macdonald*

Gradually, MacLeod and his team of young ministers built a strong
community around the facilities of the Pearce Institute:

> 'Groups were formed to assist men with PT [physical training], and
> other ways of filling in their empty days. The PT class was very
> successful, but, after a time, numbers began to fall away, and the
> assistants were sent out to find out why. Eventually, one man said he
> loved the class, but his family would go hungry if he ate all the food
> he felt he needed after the exercise.'
> – *Uist Macdonald*

MacLeod's response was simple and immediate:

'George MacLeod had the men over working in the garden at the Pearce Institute. He fed them too. And he made a workroom where they could mend their children's boots and shoes.'
– *Annie Price*

In the Pearce Institute, MacLeod and his assistants ministered to body, mind and soul. You can still hear the excitement in Annie Price's voice as she recalls those days:

'There was a big room with about a dozen big tubs where working girls – girls in service – could come on their day off and do their own washing. And we had baths as well. And there was great big dryers. And we had a canteen.

The Girls' Club had country dancing. We had keep-fit, badminton, and we had drama. We did a pantomime in 1938. I was Cinderella, and we had all the weans from Wanlock Street – they were fairies. And as well as being a leading lady, I was the front half of the coo! And the carriage for Cinderella was a Beattie's bread board.

And the pews were packed in these days. If you listened to George MacLeod, you sat on the edge of your seat he was so good. Oh yeah, he was some preacher! And Saturday night dance club was great! That was your life. And then George MacLeod bought an old mill out Barrhead way.'
– *Annie Price*

Fingleton was a disused mill which had fallen into disrepair. George MacLeod persuaded unemployed men from Govan to use their skills and their labour to make the mill habitable, so that groups from the parish could enjoy short breaks away from the city:

'George had this old bus. Everybody knew this bus. It was forever breaking down in Paisley Road on its way to Fingleton Mill. The men in the Men's Club and the boys did it up. It was big rooms, and I think it was just palliasses[4] we used to sleep on. It wasn't luxury. But they dug quite a nice wee pool, and we could go in and swim.'
– *Annie Price*

The restoration of Fingleton Mill was the culmination of MacLeod's experiment in community-building in Govan, and, in retrospect, a rehearsal for another, more daring project: the rebuilding of the Abbey on Iona, and the founding of the Iona Community:

'George thought something new was needed – an experiment – and it came down to this: why not rebuild the ancient buildings on Iona where he'd often been on holiday? As Columba had experimented in Christian living and sharing, why not get a team and go there? There were plenty of books about the Christian faith. What was needed was to see the faith in action: living it out; sharing it. That was the challenge.'
– *Uist Macdonald*

As Uist suggests, George MacLeod already knew the island of Iona well. Flora Brill used to spend every summer on Iona with her family. She remembers seeing George MacLeod there in the early 1930s:

'I had seen George MacLeod when I was a child. He seemed such a tall man to me. He used to wear shorts, and my sister's father-in-law was shocked at this.'
– *Flora Brill*

The Abbey church on Iona had been rebuilt at the turn of the 20th century, but the buildings around it were still in ruins:

'There was a Dr Russell who went to Iona every year. He owned a paper-mill, and he offered to finance the rebuilding of the outbuildings round the Abbey, but the Trustees turned him down. So the next thing was George MacLeod somehow won over the Trustees, and he went around collecting funds, and that's how it started.'
– *Flora Brill*

'Initially, it was a scheme to train young ministers through worship, work and sharing the whole of life, and to enable working men to realise that they had a vital part to play, and were needed by, and in, the Church.'
– *Uist Macdonald*

With hindsight, it is clear that the concept of a community of young ministers and craftsmen based around the Abbey on Iona was a natural progression from MacLeod's work in Govan. There, he had been able to train just a handful of assistants, and to draw a relatively small number of working men into community. On Iona, he would be able to train much larger numbers of ministers, demonstrate this new way of being Church, and put craftsmen at the very heart of communal life.

A vision shared

But it would be a mistake to believe that MacLeod's vision for Iona was his alone. In fact, he consulted with a number of people who were seeking, simultaneously, to find ways to make the Church more relevant to the lives of ordinary men and women.

Faith Aitken remembers George MacLeod's visits to her parents, Ralph and Jenny Morton, in Cambridge, in the late 1930s:

'They had just come back from China, from Manchuria, living under Japanese occupation there, and then went to Cambridge, which they found almost unreal. It was so detached from the world that they had been in. All very pleasant and very cultured, but they felt, I think, when George MacLeod came to visit, that he was one of the few people who were on the same wavelength as they were. Who were concerned about the state of the world. Concerned about industry, and the way the Church seemed to be so remote from ordinary, working people.'
– *Faith Aitken*

And Faith recalls how MacLeod would closet himself away with her parents to discuss plans for this new community:

'George came frequently to preach and give talks to students, at the time when the whole idea of an Iona Community and a team of people to rebuild the Abbey was coming together in his mind. And he was talking to our parents about it. We certainly would overhear the word "Iona" anyway, and the idea of an Iona Community. That would be … the end of 1937.'
– *Faith Aitken*

Ian Fraser also shared George Macleod's passion for a Church that could speak to ordinary people, and was in contact with him before the Iona Community came into being in 1938:

> 'I had had to work in my father's shop from the age of seven, and was aware of the gap between us – the "respectable" people – and the folk that worked in the shop, who were gathered at street corners on Sundays when the respectable people went to church. I felt I had to do something about the gap between the ordinary folk – who were the working folk that sustained the world – and the "respectables".'
> – *Ian Fraser*

Ian would become an early member of the Community, and a significant figure in the development of its thinking – as would Lex Miller:

> 'Lex was a minister in a church in Stepney [in London's East End]. And, in the same way as George was involved with Govan, Lex was involved in Stepney. They were asking the same questions. They were aware of the pressures. They were aware of the gap between the Church and the working class. So there was a very strong link there. Lex came up, and, for a while, was Deputy Leader of the Iona Community.'
> – *Douglas Trotter*

And there were others who were asking the same questions George MacLeod was asking. Some, like the Mortons and Ian Fraser, were in dialogue with him, even before the Community existed. Others, like Lex Miller, shortly after it was founded. But all were to play significant roles in the shaping of the new Community – despite the fact that they often disagreed with George MacLeod, personally:

> 'We were never called "MacLeodites"! We were not a conformist community around one man. George did really see the need for people with different emphases and different gifts to come together into a community. Okay, I'd argue with him at times, but he did see the need, and, in the end, he would bow to that need for rich and full community.'
> – *Ian Fraser*

Though seldom acknowledged, it is perhaps one of George MacLeod's greatest merits that, while autocratic by nature, he was brave enough to recruit talented people who were often very different from himself, and allow them to shape the Community. He may not have always enjoyed the experience of leading a diverse community, but by building in such diversity from the start, he guaranteed the Community's health and, ultimately, its effectiveness.

The founding of the Community

Having settled on the idea of a community of ministers and craftsmen, George MacLeod set about enlisting the ministers in a methodical way. He toured the Divinity Faculties of Scotland like a Recruiting Officer, 'selling' the vision of his new community to students. Raymond Bailey's experience was typical of those encounters:

'In the summer of my last year at university [1938], George visited New College with the purpose of appealing to New College for people to take part in this plan he had, which, as I understood it, was to come to Iona to share in both manual work and academic work – what he called "ministerial training". And to give us the chance of personal contact with uneducated tradesmen – the joiners and the masons that were beginning the work of rebuilding the ruins of Iona Abbey. We were to come for the summer, and for the next two years we were to give our time to a Church Extension minister in a Church Extension charge.[5] What he seemed to offer, particularly the manual work and the contact with tradesmen, was something that immediately attracted me.'
– *Raymond Bailey*

Bill Cooper was also a Divinity student when he signed up for summer 1939, and he too was attracted by MacLeod's description of the project:

'The Church, at one time, was at the centre of the life of the community, and we felt that it was time for the Church to mean something to people again. We were going to go into a situation that was beginning to get more and more difficult for the Church, and here was some-

thing that might put the Church back into the centre of life.'
— *Bill Cooper*

While George MacLeod was recruiting the ministers, a master mason called Bill Amos set about recruiting the craftsmen. Adam Campbell was one of the first masons to take up the challenge:

'Willie Amos had told me about the Abbey. He was a great boy for hiking, so that year [1938] he had hiked across Mull, and went to the Abbey, and was invited to a meal. And Dr MacLeod said, "Come on, I'll show you what I'm going to do." He said, "I'm going to restore this, and have students and folk up, but where will I get tradesmen? Masons? Joiners?" Willie said, "I'm a mason. I'll get masons." So he did. So that's how I came up.'
— *Adam Campbell*

Many other interviewees told this story of how Bill Amos had just happened to be hiking across Mull, had visited Iona, and had stumbled across George MacLeod, but Bill's son, Bill Amos Jnr, sees it rather differently:

'I don't think that he would have been there just by chance. You don't go to Iona, and wander off the top of a hill down towards an abbey where you can see people working. Getting to Iona was difficult. I think he knew about the project, but he was probably not convinced that he wanted to have anything to do with it. But once he saw it, and got talking, that was it. This was something that encompassed all that he wanted to do.'
— *Bill Amos*

George Wilkie, an early member of the Community, remembers Bill Amos well, and feels that his contribution to the formation of the Community has still not been fully recognised:

'Bill got together a group of workmen whom he knew on building sites in Edinburgh, and who were prepared to give up their jobs at the beginning of June [to go to Iona], knowing that they would be out of work in September. Some of them were, I suppose, nominal

Christians. One at least, if not two, were definitely Marxist, so they enlivened the conversation. But these groups were part of the Community, so that ministers were exposed to their thinking, and their way of looking at things, in a way that perhaps we haven't been since the end of the rebuilding. And I feel that I would like to underline Bill's place, almost alongside George MacLeod, because George was going round the colleges and getting young ministers, whereas Bill had to bring in the working men.'
– *George Wilkie*

And Bill's son contends that just as the young ministers were drawn to George MacLeod and his new Community for ideological reasons, so too was his father:

'I think he got involved because George MacLeod was a pacifist, and so was my father. I think he got involved because George MacLeod was a socialist. So was my father. And I think he got involved because he could see George MacLeod's religion being relevant, especially at that time. It was a meeting of minds, as much as anything else. He could empathise very much with what the objective was, and see that it was going to be something quite important.'
– *Bill Amos*

The group that master mason Bill Amos had 'stumbled across' in the summer of 1938 was a trail-blazing group of ministers and craftsmen who had come to Iona to make preparations for the rebuilding of the Abbey. Uist Macdonald, one of George MacLeod's assistants in Govan, was one of those young ministers:

'George said, "I'm going to get a team together. Will you come?" The next day, I went over and said, "I'm in on it with you, if you'll have me." So that was it. And he went on from that, and got together a team which consisted of an architect, a doctor, a secretary, seven artisans, four trained ministers, and four in training. And there we were, trying to work out the legacy of Columban Christianity.

We met together in Glasgow, and George outlined things to us, and we all got navy blue shirts and suits for formal occasions. We were

fitted out with these, and then we spent that evening and night there, and then proceeded towards Iona. As you got further down the Clyde – Port Glasgow, Greenock, and then out – it became very rough, and we had quite a nasty night of it. But, eventually, we got clear, and sailed right on to Iona. For some of them it was quite a daring experience, because some had never been on the sea before, and certainly not in the choppy stuff you can get on the west coast of Scotland.'
– *Uist Macdonald*

On arrival on Iona that very first party had to sort out their living quarters:

'On the east side of the Abbey grounds, just beneath the Abbey, we had put up a line of huts with little rooms where people could live, and in the early days, we had to finish that and get it into order, so that we could have more people there.'
– *Uist Macdonald*

'It was a long wooden building which we called the "Rome Express", and it really was very like the old railway coaches where you had little rooms off the main corridor. In each room there was a bed, there was a kind of oak-coloured chest of drawers, and a chair. Full stop. And we each got one.'
– *Douglas Trotter*

'There were 25 wonderful little rooms there in the long corridor, and you could tell by the number of steps who was visiting who.'
– *George Wilkie*

'You could hear what your neighbour was doing next door, of course, but it was wind- and watertight. Couldn't have been better!'
– *Bill Cooper*

But living in such close proximity to one another could be challenging:

'It was interesting, but difficult, because I needn't tell you that you can't walk off a wee island. You're there, and you've got to learn to live with the folk who are there, and come to terms with them, and realise that they are entitled to a viewpoint different from yours. And you

must try to understand it, and they've to try to understand yours. I think, quite apart from the things that we discussed in terms of what we were trying to do, it gave us quite useful, and sometimes remarkable, insights into the way that people tick.'
— *Uist Macdonald*

All in all, there were many encouraging signs that first year. Although the young Douglas Trotter had been invited to Iona in 1938 simply to help keep the place clean and tidy, he was allowed to attend the meetings of the original members:

'I witnessed their enthusiasm which was generated by George MacLeod. I witnessed a view of the Church and Christianity which had never dawned on me before. I mean, to me, being a Christian was going to the church on Sunday morning, and a Bible class. This interest in the Church as a vital force was totally new to me.'
— *Douglas Trotter*

Deaconess Alice Scrimgeour, who was already working in the Gallowgate, a desperately poor area of Glasgow, also happened to be on Iona during the summer of 1938, and she too was impressed by MacLeod's vision:

'It was the first summer and, of course, George came round the two hotels and all the boarding houses, and explained what he was doing. We went to this meeting in the Argyll Hotel, and were fascinated. By that time I was nearly two years in Gallowgate, and I knew that there was something not right about the Church at that time – that we weren't getting anywhere fast – although there were twelve hundred members in the church. So I was particularly interested in George saying that Govan wasn't really being a parish church, because it was ignoring the people, the poor people in the parish, and I got excited then, and I wrote him a wee letter saying I was a Church Sister in an East End church, and I was very interested.'
— *Alice Scrimgeour*

However, despite these early encouragements, things were not going entirely according to plan.

Annie Price, one of George MacLeod's parishioners, also witnessed the birth of the Community. During the summer of 1938, she camped on Iona with a group from Govan Old, and watched as the 'Rome Express' went up. But later that year, she became aware that MacLeod was facing serious problems within the Church of Scotland:

> 'There was a great stooshie,[6] because George MacLeod wanted to start the Iona Community and still remain in Govan. The powers-that-be in Govan and in the Presbytery[7] didn't want it. And there was a great hoo-ha about it. I was the younger generation then, and we had a committee – "the Pochlers"[8] – that's what they called us! We were refused a room to have a meeting in, in the Pearce Institute. Weren't allowed! We had to hire a room up in the Town Hall. And we went out and canvassed members who were willing to have him on that footing. We didn't get anywhere. George wanted to do it, and we were backing him – we were really behind him – but there were other elements that were very much agin' it. And let's face it – George didn't have a lot of backing in the Presbytery at times. The knives were out.'
> – *Annie Price*

And Annie is equally clear about the reason for MacLeod's unpopularity within Glasgow Presbytery:

> 'Och, just jealousy, of course. I'm quite sure it was. I mean he was a man that was going to make his mark no matter what he did. That was obvious.'
> – *Annie Price*

Annie may well be right: the Church of Scotland's opposition to the Iona project may well have been directed more at George MacLeod personally than at the Community. Douglas Trotter certainly believes so:

> 'My memory of these early days is that it was really anti-George, rather than anti what the Community was about. People didn't stop to think what it was about! There was more thought in the Church of Scotland about George as a person than about the principles of the Community, because he was very outspoken; because he had made a name for himself; and because he could be very acerbic, very brutal,

very critical. He didn't hesitate to call a spade a spade, and I think that that caused a lot of dislike, rather than people seriously taking what he was saying to task.'
– *Douglas Trotter*

Raymond Bailey agrees that the focus of the Church's suspicion was George MacLeod himself:

'One thing that came into it was that George MacLeod was a pacifist, and the other was that he was a member of the Labour Party. And the Church in general, in those days, certainly wasn't pacifist. And it wasn't Labour.'
– *Raymond Bailey*

However, there were concerns within the Church about the fledgling Community too:

'There were great misgivings and a lot of doubts about these young ministers "aping" George MacLeod. I was interested in everything he had to say, because it seemed to me to ring true. I really must confess I became a minister because I wanted to join the Community, rather than the other way about. And there was a great deal of worry about this.'
– *George Wilkie*

'In the early years we got a lot of kicks. We were thought of as weird. The word "Communism" was used as well, because of the concern for politics, and for aiming at justice in the world. I don't think people realise how dismissive some folk were of politicised church people in the early days. Justice as a general idea was favoured, of course. But you hadn't to be too particular, and the Iona Community was quite particular.'
– *Ian Fraser*

'The Community was also accused of being next door to Rome! The Roman Catholic allegation was probably because of the introduction of responses and corporate participation in worship. So much of Presbyterian worship had become the minister standing in the pulpit and talking, and talking, and talking, and the idea that we would have

responses, that people would participate, was thought of as Roman.'
– *Stewart McGregor*

However, MacLeod had, to some extent, foreseen these problems, and
had attempted to arm the Community with a number of sponsors who
were unimpeachable in the eyes of the Church of Scotland establishment
– among them the 'Father of the Church', former Moderator John White:

> 'George, somehow or other, had managed to get a number of people
> to act as "Trustees", I think he called them. One was John White, and
> if John White was on your side, there couldn't be much wrong with
> you. John White, who was an absolute Protestant with a capital "P",
> was yet willing to be a Trustee. Maybe John White just wanted to
> keep his hand in the pie, and make sure that it went the right way!'
> – *George Wilkie*

And, sure enough, John White did, eventually, take a stand against George
MacLeod, and the young Community found itself fighting for its life.

Ian Fraser describes their treatment at the hands of the Church of Scotland establishment:

> 'Well, I think the first word I'd use is "rough". This is partly because of
> John White's determination that there shouldn't be any kind of "loose
> and broken men", as they used to be called in the Highlands, pretend-
> ing to belong to the Church, and not really belonging to the Church.'
> – *Ian Fraser*

It was a struggle to find a form of association which would be acceptable
to both the Church of Scotland and the Community:

> 'George with his strong constitutional sense wanted to make sure that
> this was not just a kind of voluntary association of people with a
> special bee in their bonnet. And he worked hard at this, until they got
> an arrangement that even John White was prepared to acknowledge,
> where the Community reports to the General Assembly.'
> – *Ian Fraser*

But even after the constitutional arrangements of the new Community had been sorted out, more or less to everyone's satisfaction, its members were still regarded with suspicion by many in the Church:

> 'I got the impression that the wider Church thought of the Iona Community as a slightly dodgy, heterodox, rabble-rousing group – disturbers of the peace.'
> – *Richard Holloway*

> 'I remember when I was applying for my parishes, I put down I was a member of the Community, and as I wrote, I thought, "This might be a black mark with certain people." There was no question of hiding it, but I think one just was known as an "Iona person".'
> – *Douglas Trotter*

> '"Iona Men" couldn't get jobs. They couldn't get parishes, because they were Iona people.'
> – *David Jarvie*

And it wasn't just the Church of Scotland establishment who had questions about the young Community. The islanders too were wary:

> 'When we started, some of them were a bit suspicious: Who are these folk? What are they really going to do on the island? Are some of the things that they're suggesting really necessary? But we went out in twos and visited the homes of the island, and generally were given a very friendly reception. I had a great advantage, being a Highlander and an islander, and having a bit of Gaelic at my command. So I got to know the island people, and was willingly accepted into their homes.'
> – *Uist Macdonald*

Other members of the Community, however, including George MacLeod, were less successful than Uist in forming good relationships with the local people and, despite his efforts, a significant number of islanders remained wary of the incomers at the Abbey. It would be a continuing source of sadness for some members of the Iona Community for many years to come.

The organisation of the Community: 'a well-ordered day'

Once the whole team had been assembled on Iona, William Fallon and his wife, Dinah, who had looked after George MacLeod when he lived in the Pearce Institute in Govan, came to look after the men:

'Fallon had been George MacLeod's batman in the army, and he followed George to Iona, and he still looked after George. But Dinah was the boss. Dinah was a great big, sturdy mama who ruled the roost, and did the cooking, and you kept on the right side of Dinah.'
– *Douglas Trotter*

For Ian Renton who, like many of the other early members, had served in the forces, it was a regime he was more than comfortable with:

'I'd been in the army and was accustomed to men's company. This was not dissimilar because, for our meals, we all sat round one table, and there was a lot of banter went on, and teasing.'
– *Ian Renton*

Soon a pattern of work, worship and relaxation was established:

'We got up in the morning with a bell, I remember, and we had breakfast in a common room which was at the end of the "Rome Express". After breakfast, we then went across to the Abbey for morning prayers.'
– *Douglas Trotter*

'By eight o'clock we were in the Abbey, the workmen in their dungarees, and us in our blue trousers and jerseys. And we were there worshipping for not more than twenty minutes – probably more like quarter of an hour. And then the minister members had a Bible study.'
– *George Wilkie*

'Until lunchtime we discussed the Church, and we discussed what we were doing as a Community. After lunch, we joined the craftsmen for jobs. Now you didn't become a mason overnight, but you helped with this and that, gathered slates. And your time was spent learning a

little about how the workers of the world saw themselves.'
– *Douglas Trotter*

'You helped by getting cement. We had the use of a horse and cart, and we dumped it at the east end of the Abbey. And we worked from there, mixing cement, and taking part as fairly unskilled labourers with journeymen builders and masons. We just had to pitch in. And I must say that, by the end of the day, you felt as if you had been pitching in, because a student or a minister, until he went to Iona, hadn't been doing a great deal of hard physical work.'
– *Uist Macdonald*

'And then there was always a meeting in the evening, a gathering on some subject or some issue of the day, where all were together, and that was where you did recognise the difference between ministers and workmen. But you did all contribute, and some of the workmen were very articulate. So it was not a one-way process by any means.'
– *George Wilkie*

'And then we finished up by going back to prayers in the Abbey.'
– *Douglas Trotter*

'It was a very well-ordered day. And there was a great feeling of doing things together. There was a tremendous spirit.'
– *George Wilkie*

Contrary to popular myth, none of the craftsmen was drawn from the ranks of the unemployed, and John Sim remembers with affection the skilled men for whom he laboured:

'All the different trades were represented there, and they were all men who had chosen to come to Iona to do this job, almost as a calling I would say. They were men who had a great compassion for these idiots who could hardly tell their right hand from their left. We spent our lives with them. We all ate together, we all worshipped together, we all played football together, and we all had conferences together. It was a very full and meaningful fellowship.'
– *John Sim*

But not every group of ministers and craftsmen bonded successfully. Raymond Bailey reports that, in 1939, he found himself forced to 'take sides':

'I became friendly with three of the tradesmen: Jim Lawson, Bill Amos and Adam Campbell, and this lasted after we'd left Iona. Once, I happened to be standing near a small group of tradesmen, and they were talking about their relationship with the ministers. I was near enough for them to include me, and they said something about the fact that the ministers never seemed to make any contact with them. At least, that was the gist of it, and I said, rather self-righteously, "Well, I don't think that's true of me. I've been friendly with some of you." "Aye, and see what you've done? You've cut yourself off from the ministers."'

– Raymond Bailey

But, over time, ministers and craftsmen clearly developed mutual respect:

'We got on fine – after a bit. We got pally with some – well, I got pally with Graham [Raymond] Bailey. Kept in touch with him even when he was abroad, and I was abroad. And we kept in touch ever since. We got on fine with Uist [Macdonald] and big Mac – big Hamish MacIntyre. We were in the puffer[9] once, and the skipper was quite impressed with Hamish. Wouldnae believe he was a minister. He said, "Ach well, if he cannae get a kirk, he can get a job wi' me."'

– Adam Campbell

John Young, who was an apprentice joiner when he was recruited to work on the Abbey, remembers the bonds forged by worshipping together:

'Oh, the impressive thing, as far as I was concerned, was that you were sitting in a choir stall with other craftsmen and the ministers – the members of the Community. So it was a real community: a mixture of people, all there with different ideas, and different purposes. I cannot really remember the text, or some of the things that were being spoken about, but just the whole "feeling". To me, it illustrated what a real community could be like.'

– John Young

That sense of community seems to have extended to the members' free time too:

> 'There was some little leisure in the evening where we would relax a bit, or discuss things, or get to know more about the craftsmen. They were always interesting. One of the lads was a bit of a communist, his name was MacNaughton. I could hear him arguing with Dr MacLeod many a time, saying, "It's all right for you!" This kind of thing. And it was interesting to hear what they were thinking about, and what life was like as workmen in these days. They weren't specially chosen, these men. They weren't hand-picked. They volunteered to come to Iona. It was perhaps a little odd that some of them would want to, because some of them had never had any experience of the Church at all. But it was interesting to hear their attitudes towards the clergy, and towards what we were doing. That was good for us: to know that religion was something that mattered, for them, as well as for us. Knowing them was good.'
> *– Bill Cooper*

At the end of the summer, the Community dispersed, most of the craftsmen to look for work in their home towns, and the ministers to a parish:

> 'When the summer was over, the ministers were sent to various parishes that were willing to have someone from Iona, and they went there and worked as assistant ministers.'
> *– Uist Macdonald*

Originally, they were expected to spend two years in the parish of an Iona Community member, or at least of someone sympathetic to the Community. Mainly, these were city parishes in areas of social deprivation or parishes which had been created under the Church Extension Scheme. There, they would put into practice the emphases which they had learned and 'lived' on Iona. But how did those early Iona Community ministers view the prospect of working in these challenging parishes?

> 'It was always being said that the Church didn't count for much any more. It was on the sidelines. Nobody got very much out of the Church any more. Numbers were declining. And here was a challenge

that I think we all wanted to have a share in. You know, roll up the sleeves and try to get people back into the fold, as it were. But, more than that, to get people to see that religion was something that dealt with the whole of life, not just a Sunday.'
— *Bill Cooper*

And that sense of Community Men being on the front-line of the Church's work and witness persisted throughout the first 30 years of the Community's life. Ian Whyte was a 'New Man' in the 1960s:

'I suppose we saw ourselves as pioneers. We were going to where the real stuff was! I think we probably had a bit of a conceit about ourselves in a way. There was certainly a feeling – and I think it's persisted until quite recently – that to be "real" in the ministry, you had to go to an Iona Community parish, and the more socially deprived the better – or the more pioneering, if it was a Church Extension parish.'
— *Iain Whyte*

What wasn't immediately clear to the early members, however, was what membership of the Iona Community might mean at the end of their two-year 'apprenticeship':

'I was asking George MacLeod, what did he see after two years? What happens? Because we were only to go to our jobs under the Community for two years, and then we'd look for a parish. Do what we liked. And he said, "Well, I don't see this becoming the Community. It will only go on as long as God requires it." He did give me the impression, and I don't think I'm misrepresenting him, that he saw us going and setting up a community within the parish, similar to the one on Iona, and that there might be a bit of a connection between the two, but that was where the Community was to exist – not on Iona. I think this is quite an important point. Iona was the example. It was the place where you tried it out, and saw how it worked, and what the difficulties were, but the real community had to be in the parish. So I don't think that George anticipated the Community becoming the sort of continuing organisation it has become.'
— *George Wilkie*

Given that the roots of George MacLeod's vision for the Community sprang from his experience as a Church of Scotland minister, he is unlikely to have predicted a continuing Community comprising both lay and ordained people, drawn from many denominations. Nor, given his preoccupation with training ministers, did he anticipate that women would ever become part of the Community:

> 'Well, George was very gracious to women, and didn't want them anywhere near the Community. He thought that the basis of Gospel announcement had to do with clergy: male clergy in dog collars. Not that it needed to be dog collars all the time, but it was "the dog-collared" who were the advance guard of the Church.'
> – *Ian Fraser*

And since the Church of Scotland did not, at that time, recognise women clergy, the Community was also, by definition, an all-male community:

> 'In those days the idea of women ministers just hadn't arisen. Mary, my wife, wanted to be one, and tried, but they just said gently, "Well, you can come and train, but the Church won't accept you."'
> – *Raymond Bailey*

At first, this presented no problem to George MacLeod. Women's expectations, on the whole, were limited:

> 'There were women who were very happy to be working in various ancillary roles, but most of them had no imagination of the possibility of them being members of the Community. They knew perfectly well that this was the male prerogative. And they were perfectly happy to leave it at that, to be quite honest.'
> – *John Sim*

But, in those very early days, few of the young members of the Community had wives:

> 'It was an all-male Community and, first of all, a bachelors' Community. And then, of course, people started getting married, and I do remember George MacLeod saying to me, "This raises questions

about the Community's existence."'
– *George Wilkie*

Indeed, it did. The bachelor Community had, over a number of years, developed a Rule by which they promised to live. Some aspects of that discipline were uncontentious; but others had far-reaching implications for the wives and children of members:

'It was a discipline of personal devotions, Bible study and prayer. And there was an economic discipline, where there was an attempt being made to encourage all of us to live as near as possible to the working-class level, and to make a contribution of a certain proportion of our disposable income towards Community efforts and other charities.'
– *John Sim*

One of the main influences in the development of the Economic Discipline was Lex Miller. Tony Gibson, who was later to produce radio programmes about the Community for the BBC, met Lex Miller when he was working in the East End of London during the Blitz:

'Lex was the minister resident for "St Paul's on the Highway" in Shadwell. Very down-to-earth, and thinking hard about what needed to be done, who needed to do it, and where it needed to be done. They were setting up what were then called "Rest Centres" which was where people came in the daytime when the raids were not happening, and you constantly brewed up vast jugs of coffee and soup.'
– *Tony Gibson*

Tony Gibson admired Lex's thoroughness and his eye for detail, as he organised food and accommodation for bombed-out Stepney residents – talents which he later applied within the Community to the drafting of guidelines for mutual accountability for financial expenditure:

'Lex wrote a very good pamphlet on how you go about setting up a Minimum Wage Group. And I think it was that that probably helped the Community back on Iona to get its act together in that respect.'
– *Tony Gibson*

But when the members of the 'Bachelor Community' began to get married, it was not immediately obvious that their wives would be happy to go along with Lex's careful calculations, especially as they were prohibited from playing any part in the Community's decision-making process. David Levison joined the Community in 1943, and went, with his wife, Cecilia, to St John's, Perth where they replaced two departing Community members, Bob Craig and Bill Smith:

> 'Oh, I think one definitely felt excluded. One wasn't a real person somehow or other. In those days, for our economic discipline, we more or less had to give an account for what we spent during the week, and I remember being quite taken aback one time, when Lex Miller spoke up, and, with a twinkle in his eye, said, "These Levisons have been a bit extravagant. They've been out for a meal!" And this was a wedding anniversary as far as I remember! But, in those days, we carefully noted everything, and we saw that our proportion to church and other giving was always there.'
> – *Cecilia Levison*

Community members working in economically deprived areas found that the economic discipline put an extra pressure on their marriage:

> 'If you are a bachelor, it's easy. When you have to involve your wife in it, the economic discipline is a different story. I found it very difficult, because 10% of my income wasn't 10% of George MacLeod's income, because he had a vast fortune. I felt that hard, because, in London, my salary was £620 a year. Three children, no car, and I received very few expenses. And, therefore, I did find that very difficult! I probably didn't live up to it properly.'
> – *Ian Renton*

In the end, it was the stringencies of the economic discipline that set in motion the slow process by which women became part of the Community. It wasn't that the wives were unwilling to live sacrificially: they were, and they did. But the sense of alienation, of something which so profoundly affected their lives being decided by a process which they could never hope to influence, created an ever-increasing demand for personal involvement in the decision-making forums of the Community.

John Sim explains:

'Those of us who were in the position where they had no money at all, except their stipend, which very often in those days was three months, if not six months, behind time, were living from hand to mouth in a real sense. There was no possibility of any of us ever having an overdraft. Bank managers said, "If you give a minister an overdraft, he'll never pay it off."

I think a number of wives really felt, "This is all very well, these men laying down the law, making the rules, but we're the ones who've got to cope with the actual challenge of this. We want a say in this matter as well." And after a comparatively short time, it became obvious that there was a demand for Family Groups to meet and discuss Community issues. And so they set up Family Groups in various parts of the country, where ministers and their wives met together, and discussed all kinds of issues, including the Economic Discipline.

Now that was the beginning. That was the impetus for change. Some of the ministers' wives became quite concerned to have a larger share in Community thinking, and although many of them didn't actually become members, they became quite influential in the background. And, of course, after I had ceased to be a member of the Community, this impetus grew, and I think probably, over the years, there have been more women members of the Iona Community than men, coming from all kinds of backgrounds and nationalities.'
– *John Sim*

And so the first clearly identifiable phase of Community life was over. The wild child of Scottish church life was now a mature, if not quite respectable, grown-up.

1

2

3

4

5

6

9

10

Photos

1. George MacLeod's mode of dress (left) shocked the islanders (Faith Aitken archive)

2. Members of the 1939 Community: Back row, left to right: Bill Cooper, Uist Macdonald, Hamish MacIntyre, Ralph Morton, Jimmy Currie. Front row, left to right: Bobby Ross, Johnny MacMillan, George MacLeod, Cameron Wallace, Ian Fraser (Bill Cooper archive)

3. Lex Miller with George MacLeod, 1944 (Ian Fraser archive)

4. Master mason, Bill Amos (Raymond Bailey archive)

5. Mason Adam Campbell dressing stone for the Abbey (Raymond Bailey archive)

6. Huts were erected on the east side of the Abbey (Raymond Bailey archive)

7. The huts became known as the 'Rome Express' (Duncan Finlayson archive)

8. Douglas Trotter kept the 'Rome Express' clean and tidy (Duncan Finlayson archive)

9. Dinah and William Fallon (Raymond Bailey archive)

10. Raymond Bailey working on the roof, 1939 (Raymond Bailey archive)

The Community and young people

Despite the fact that Govan Old had had a thriving Boys' Club and Girls' Club throughout George MacLeod's ministry there, youth work does not seem to have figured in his original plans for Iona:

> 'When George was at this early stage of the Community, people said, "There's something here that's terribly important for young people. Are you going to do work among young people?" And he said, "That's a huge field. If the Community gets drawn aside into getting involved with young people, it'll be a complete disaster."'
> – *Duncan Finlayson*

Consequently, the earliest incarnation of the Community's youth work seems to have derived from the central concern of the Community to make the Christian faith relevant to the lives of the urban poor:

> 'The Community's emphasis at that time was on what was called "Industrial Mission" – a mission to the working classes who seemed to have been excluded from the Church. And as part of that mission, they set up the "Christian Workers' League" [CWL], which was based on a Roman Catholic youth organisation, "Jeunesse Ouvrière Chréti-enne", started by a Cardinal Cardijn in Belgium.'
> – *Jack Kellet*

> 'George MacLeod had been very concerned about the fact that Boys' Clubs were really just places for taking poor boys off the streets. He felt that it ought to be an organisation helping young people to relate to the world about them in a conscious way, and a socially concerned way. So he and John Summers attended a conference of "Young Christian Workers" [in Birmingham at Easter 1941], and John got the job of starting up "Jeunesse Ouvrière Chrétienne" – or a group like it – in Canongate, which in those days was the headquarters of the Community in Edinburgh. John managed to contact a couple of boys, and they contacted others, and by the second year of their existence they had about eight to ten members. I went down, after it had been going for about six months. I was just a hanger-on, but I was helping John in whatever way I could. In fact, we divided into two groups, and I was an Advisor in one, and he was in the other. It had all the fun of a club,

but the central event in it was a study of some social problem.'
– *George Wilkie*

The club met formally for the first time on 4th January 1942, and, initially, they had three club evenings a week. On Sunday, they had speakers and discussions. On Wednesday, they had gym. But Friday night was Action Night.

Jack Kellet, who joined CWL in 1946 when he was just 17 years old, describes the order of events on Friday evenings:

> 'CWL had formulated this pattern for their investigations which was "See", "Judge" and "Act". In "See", you had to find out facts about a matter of social concern like housing. Then there was a section called "Judge", which was trying to draw on lessons from scripture. And then you weren't allowed to complete the evening without "Action". Now the Action might be that you were going to write, that night, to the Secretary of State for Scotland. The Secretary of State must have got fed up with these letters coming out of the Canongate! So here was a Bible-based organisation learning about the world, and how Christians should judge and act within it.'
> – *Jack Kellet*

One of the first things the boys decided – just three months after the club was founded – was that it should be open to girls. In that respect, they were 'Seeing, Judging and Acting' with greater insight than the Community itself at that time: it took the Iona Community 30 years to reach the decision to admit women:

> 'John Summers was marvellous, and when they decided that they wanted girls in, he said, "I don't agree with it, but if you want it, it's your decision." And so girls came in.'
> – *George Wilkie*

One of the first girls to come through the doors was 17-year-old Peggy Bee:

> 'They were looking for workers – industrial workers. One of the problems was that Youth Fellowships were mainly filled with middle-class

– they weren't filled with working-class children. We never had any more than eight people in the group, and although we had somebody called an Advisor at the side, they never spoke, unless we wanted. I don't know how they managed to do that!'
– *Peggy Bee*

Among the first female Advisors to be recruited by John Summers was a young teacher, Joan Low:

'I was a primary school teacher, teaching in the Canongate, and John Summers was the School Chaplain. I knew him quite well: I'd been to his home and met his parents. It was a privileged background – he'd been at Edinburgh Academy and Oxford – but he was a serious-minded man who wanted to help to change things. He came one day and asked if I would come to his youth club to teach country dancing, and that's how I got involved in Christian Workers' League.'
– *Joan Low*

At first, the club had the use of a room and a gym in the local school, but then they found more permanent premises:

'John Summers got the first floor flat in a condemned building that had been empty for maybe twenty or more years – 179 Canongate – just up from the Tolbooth. And we did it up ourselves – I remember I painted all the doors. We knocked three rooms into one, and then we had a club! From that point, we started to really do things.'
– *Peggy Bee*

'They did all sorts of things actually. Went to see owners of property to ask why they weren't doing something about the drains; took up questions with the trades unions about youth employment, and apprenticeships, and so on.'
– *George Wilkie*

'I can remember a deaconess of the Church of Scotland coming and telling us about the number of people living in great loneliness and considerable distress, and members of the Christian Workers' League, including Ena [Jack's future wife] and Joan Low, who was

one of our Advisors, going out to people who were living in very poor circumstances to cut their nails, and scrub the stairs, and things like that.'
– *Jack Kellet*

Ena Kellet, then just 14, lived in a tenement in the High Street, and had joined CWL at her mother's insistence:

'Joan and I visited lots of houses in the Canongate. I thought the room-and-kitchen I lived in was pretty awful, but some of them were a million times worse, especially for elderly pensioners who couldn't get out and about.'
– *Ena Kellet*

'Certain stairs and tenements were really shocking, both in the Canongate and also in the Colinton Road district behind, which is now demolished. Climbing up stairs with outside or communal lavatories, unlit stairs, and noisy stairs – all of that was shocking to me. And yet that was just the regular homes of some of the people. They had overcrowding, and problems of employment and unemployment that, again, I didn't know about. That was an important learning experience for me.'
– *Joan Low*

'At that time, tuberculosis was the real menace in society, and Ena and I used to go into this ward to visit a woman who had absolutely no visitors. Her marriage had collapsed, and she got TB, and she was fading away. The doctors were aghast that young people should be coming into the ward and exposing themselves to TB, and they were against it. But we went in every Sunday afternoon to see her, and she began to put lipstick on, and have a fresh cardigan on, and she began to look forward, because she had visitors coming in every Sunday. So that was the kind of thing that got us involved in the Iona Community, and it really changed our lives.'
– *Jack Kellet*

The young people also got the chance to visit Iona for the first time in 1942 – and it too proved to be a life-changing experience:

'Seven boys cycled from Craignure[10] with John Summers. The bikes arrived in Iona, tied together with string at all sorts of places – they were second-hand bikes. They had about nine punctures on the way! They enjoyed a week's camping in a barn opposite Achabhaich, which was, at that time, Duncan MacArthur's house, and cycled back. How they got back, I don't know. And that, I always claim, was the first Community camp on Iona.'
– *George Wilkie*

During wartime, Iona was in a Restricted Area, so it was no mean feat to take the CWL members there. Permits had to be obtained, and the journey was difficult:

'Remember, you had to get passes to go to Iona in these days. And that was one of the problems, getting their photographs and all the rest of it, to get them ready for getting them through in Oban. But it was an adventure. You were going away to the back of beyond: Iona was still a crofting community.'
– *George Wilkie*

An annual camp on Iona quickly became part of the pattern of the CWL year. Peggy Bee vividly recalls her first visit to the island:

'You went for a week to Iona during the July Trades [holiday week], because most of the boys were engineers, or electricians, and things like that. And that would be my first meeting with the Iona Community. The first year I went, we girls stayed in Iona Cottage, and the boys stayed in the school. No electric light. No hot water. But that didn't bother me, because I didn't have any hot water at home.

I remember we were invited up to the Community for tea. Sir James Lithgow had come in his yacht, with the family, and I remember washing the dishes with James Lithgow's family – which didn't faze me, funnily enough. And certainly we got to know people in the Community.'
– *Peggy Bee*

It wasn't until after the war, however, that CWL really took off. When, in

1945, John Summers went to work in Nigeria, someone else had to be found to lead CWL. George MacLeod's eye fell on the young student who had so faithfully assisted John Summers:

> 'When I had become a member of the Community, I said, "Now I just want to go into an ordinary parish – Church Extension or downtown – and serve as an ordinary minister." And George MacLeod said, "Well, John Summers who started the Christian Workers' League is going as a missionary to Africa. You'll take over there." This was nothing like what I wanted to do. Nevertheless, I'm glad. At that point, the CWL was ready for expansion. We had about ten in various Community parishes throughout the country, from Dumfries to Dundee.'
> – *George Wilkie*

Simultaneously, during that immediate post-war period, Iona Community Youth Camps came into being, and George Wilkie was involved in their inception and development too, though, again, not entirely by choice:

> 'When I took over from John Summers, he had arranged with Jimmy Currie [Community Assistant in the Old Kirk, West Pilton] that CWL and the Old Kirk youth club would camp on his uncle's farm in Arran, but I had to run it, because John was away. After that, we thought, "We must do this again," but then Jimmy was leaving, and it was a bit uncertain. So then George MacLeod said he wanted to start Youth Camps on Iona. He asked us to take one month each. Jimmy Currie would take July, and I would take August. We said, "Okay, but we're looking for a place for our youth clubs." "Oh, you can have the first week," said George. So that was fine. So, in 1946 we started, and we got the first week with the CWL and the Old Kirk youth club. And that was all right for that year.'
> – *George Wilkie*

By the next year, however, George MacLeod had been so impressed by the success of the 1946 Youth Camps that he wasn't willing to allocate a week to CWL, despite the fact that they had provided the inspiration – and the model – for Community-run village camps:

'So I said, "Okay, CWL will run its own camp at the North End." And I ran a camp that summer [1947] at Lagandorain, which is the croft where the bunkhouse is now on Iona. It was a Mr and Mrs Campbell who ran it in these days. Well, what a job I had to get all these tents up. There were no cars on the island, but John Moffat was the cook at that time, and he had the [Community] lorry, so he gave me a loan of it, and I drove all our stuff, including an old, thrown-out cooker – coal-fired cooker – and took it up to the North End. I had no idea what I was going to cook on, apart from that. I got it there about eleven o'clock at night, but I couldn't get the lorry started again, so I had to just leave it there and go to bed. John Moffat came up the next morning, and he just put two bits of wire together. He said, "Do you not know just to look under the seat and put the wires together?"'
– *George Wilkie*

Camping at the North End was always a challenge, but how much more so in 1947, when travel was restricted and food rationing was still very much in place:

'Una Murray [one of the CWL Advisors] was asked by George Wilkie to be responsible for the cooking. She didn't know what she'd be cooking on, but there would be forty kids and leaders to be fed, whatever the weather was like. George had, fortunately, found an old range, and I have this vision of Una organising us all to do the chores. And cooking pancakes! One day, there was rain, and the pancakes were being cooked on the top of this old, black stove, and the rain was splattering on it. These leaders were just phenomenally committed to the young people of what was a very depressed area.'
– *Jack Kellet*

The inner-city kids who made up the membership of CWL also struggled at first with the realities of camping on Iona:

'The young people had no experience of living in the country, certainly no experience of living on an island, so it was a tremendous eye-opener to everybody. Going for walks was certainly not part of their pattern, and they weren't equipped for it. The girls were all in high-heeled shoes, and that doesn't do on Iona. But we certainly

attended the morning and evening services in the Abbey, and I think it was a life-changing experience for people.'
– *Joan Low*

George Wilkie freely admits that he gave the young people no choice about attending services in the Abbey:

'They attended morning and evening service. I made it absolutely a strict rule that they did, and I think the result was that they got used to the Abbey, and responses, and singing, and all sorts of discussions.

George MacLeod taking services in the Abbey is something which is unforgettable, and very impressive. Not for the preaching only, but for the way that the services were dramatic performances which you were taking part in. They responded exceedingly well. And, of course, there was the usual flood of tears when they left on the Saturday morning. I think it must have made a very significant difference to their daily life.'
– *George Wilkie*

Not that it was always easy to get the campers to the Abbey: some were more interested in attending the dance in the village hall than in attending worship:

'The girls were all sitting in the tents with their rollers in, and George Wilkie came round, and said, "Come on! Time to get down to the Abbey." And we said to him, "We're no' going. We have to keep our rollers in. We're going to the dance tonight." And George said, "You are going!"

In the end, we went, and it was special, and something touched us all – and we went to the dance afterwards!'
– *Ena Kellet*

Ena's husband, Jack, also remembers the impact of worship in the Abbey during that week on Iona in 1947:

'The first thing that struck us was that it was a piano. There was no organ. And I don't know if I'd ever heard Bach played before in my life, but we found ourselves gathering there early, before the service, the sun gleaming through the great east window and reflecting off the silver Iona cross. The sound of a Bach fugue, and the singing, and the sound of George MacLeod's voice – it was just profoundly moving, and it spoke to us. All of us were deeply moved by a sense of worship which we'd never really known before – a deep sense of worship – and it helped us to grow in commitment.'

– *Jack Kellet*

For Peggy Bee, it was the Thursday evening Service of Commitment that left an indelible mark:

'I liked going forward and kneeling. And I always remember how George MacLeod would go round everyone. I've never forgotten that he gave me the text, "You are the salt of the earth". I believe in the priesthood of all believers. Now, I learned that from Iona. And I think that's terribly important.'

– *Peggy Bee*

But the full impact of the Iona experience did not hit Ena Kellet till the very end of that week:

'When I realised that Iona was a special place was on the way home. We got off the train in Edinburgh, and it was a very hot July night, about ten o'clock. I had a wee cardboard case, and I was walking down the High Street. At that time, the pubs used to be closing – and there were lots of pubs down the Royal Mile – and the drunks were all being tipped out, and the smell of booze, and the fighting, and the screaming, and the yelling! And even although I was quite young – 15 or 16 – it made me realise that there was a different way to live. It was important, that Iona experience.'

– *Ena Kellet*

In retrospect, it's clear that both CWL camps and club activities changed the course of people's lives. Jack Kellet went on to higher education and the ministry of the Church of Scotland. He and Ena were to share a pioneering ministry in the new housing scheme of Menzieshill in Dundee.

Once her children were at school, Ena went back to school herself, and got the qualifications she needed to train as a Home Economics teacher.

Peggy Bee later worked full-time for CWL, and went on to lead many Iona Community Youth Camps. Later, she worked in a university laboratory where she was a committed trade unionist. All three attribute the choices they made, and the opportunities they enjoyed, to the life-changing experience of CWL:

'I learned a lot: I learned to cook, I learned how to iron, I learned how to talk, and I met my husband there! And it was a place where I became more confident, I suppose, and less afraid.'
– *Ena Kellet*

'I think the thing I learned from CWL was how to chair a meeting: not to talk myself, but to get other people to contribute. And when we got the Union in the university, I sat on the committee that looked at the secretaries and the clerical workers. I was interested and involved in the working conditions for secretaries and clerical workers, and I would never have done that if I hadn't been to Iona and Christian Workers' League.'
– *Peggy Bee*

'It was the most important thing in our lives, belonging to the Christian Workers' League. But we were aware that there were other Christian groups whom we thought were "pie in the sky" and didn't care tuppence about other people; who thought that the Church really existed to help them live their lives, and not to help other people live their lives. We got fed up with what we regarded as their smugness and their lack of concern about what was really wrong with the world. The Gospel had to be proclaimed and lived out, outside the safe place. Our business was to change the conditions for the people of the world who couldn't. It was to bring God's Kingdom on earth.'
– *Jack Kellet*

But when George Wilkie tries to assess the success of the CWL experiment, 60 years on, he does so with some ambivalence:

'The problem about it was that these youngsters all became so able that they moved out of the working class. For instance, in my group in Port Glasgow, I had about half a dozen lads and a few girls. And three of the lads went to Ruskin College in Oxford: one of them ran a company of five hundred people for the latter part of his life; another has just retired from being a Senior Lecturer at Strathclyde [University].'
– *George Wilkie*

But, whatever George feels now, there is no doubt that CWL helped to reconnect working-class young people with the Church, and turned them into socially and politically aware adults.

And that 1947 CWL North End camp left another, very tangible legacy:

'During that week, George MacLeod came up to have a meal with us, and he said, "Oh, we must start camps at the North End!" So, although we only had that one week there, the North End camps, which were under canvas, went on from there. And, thereafter, they had their own leadership. So that's the origin of the Iona Youth Camps.'
– *George Wilkie*

So, from 1948 onwards, the Community organised its own Youth Camps on Iona, both in the village and under canvas at the North End of the island. Stewart McGregor used to help with the logistics of both camps:

'I used to finish my degree exams and go up to Iona with one or two others, and set up the camps. We'd pitch the tents at the North End: a marquee with tables in it where we lunched, the tents for the girls down at the foot of the field, and the tents for the boys up over the other side of the road. We cleaned out the bothy where the cooking was done, and we cleaned out the byre which was the only untented, solid shelter when the weather was really inclement. We'd great fun.

The village camp was probably the most sedate of the camps. I think the people who went to the village were people who probably felt they didn't want to camp at the North End. It was not nearly so exposed. We didn't have to rough it in the village.'
– *Stewart McGregor*

Stewart McGregor may have thought the village camp 'sedate', but it's not the first adjective that comes to mind when former village campers from the 1940s and '50s describe their living conditions:

'We were staying in Iona Cottage, the cottage that faces the jetty. I can't remember how many girls were in there. If I remember correctly, it was three-tier bunks: quite a crowd packed into each room.'
– *Marion Jack*

'There was no electricity then. There wasn't any running water: you just did all the washing in the sea. And there was no light: it was all paraffin lamps and some candles. There were no proper toilets: they used these chemical toilets called Elsans. I've got a photograph of somebody walking down to the jetty – they used to say, "Taking Elsie for a walk," but it was carrying down the waste matter. And it just went into Pot Washers' Bay!

Do you know where the Post Office is now? Well, opposite, there is a big green hut. That was where we had our meals. And straight across from there was Roseneath Cottage. Muriel Morton was the cook, and she did all the cooking from there, and then the food came down to that hut.'
– *Margaret Hughes*

'We all had to take turns of pumping the water in Roseneath Cottage. There was this great big handle, attached to the wall, and it took two of us, one on either side. We had to go back and forward, and back and forward, and you seemed to be going on for an hour, and the water would only have risen by half an inch. However, it had to be done. When I look back on it, it didn't seem like you were on holiday, but you were.'
– *Isobel Blair*

Even the journey to Iona was less than appealing:

'The journey was long. You stayed in Glasgow overnight, and then you set off. I think we got a train from Queen Street.'
– *Margaret Hughes*

'Then the train was always stopping, because there was a cow on the line, or something like that. We got to Oban about half-past five in the morning, and we'd wait for the "King George" steamer at nine o'clock.'
– *Jack Kellet*

'The "King George V" sailed right round, and up Mull, and into the Sound of Iona, and it was often very, very rough. Lots of people were very sick.'
– *Margaret Hughes*

'We were hardly out of the harbour when we were called down to lunch, and we'd never seen anything like this! There was fresh salmon on all the plates – which we'd never seen. I mean, salmon came out of a tin! And here was this fresh salmon with salad, and tomatoes, and so on. We couldn't believe it – and we tucked in. Then suddenly, through the porthole, we saw, one minute, the sun or the sky, and the next minute, the bed of the ocean! We were all violently ill, and spent the whole journey hanging over the side, with every-body commiserating with each other. And then the shout went up, "There's Iona!" And through the mist was this grey, absolutely unat-tractive place, but all we wanted to do was to get our feet on land.'
– *Jack Kellet*

'And when you got there, there was this quite perilous arrival, because down below you there were these little red boats, just rowing boats really, and you had to get from this great big steamer down a kind of stepladder into the little boats which were going up and down, and up and down. And then when you got into the boats, you sailed in to the jetty. And then, of course, it was a case of getting out of the little red boats.'
– *Margaret Hughes*

'We were landed on the old jetty, and walked up to the village where we all went to bed right away. But then we were, almost immediately, hauled up, because at that time there was a service every Sunday morning broadcast on the radio from the Abbey. Reggie Barrett-Ayres was the Music Master and the BBC man was Ronnie Falconer. And we were taken up there to practise the hymns for the next morning. Oh,

we were all absolutely disgusted with what was required of us. It was a most unpleasant thing.'
– *Jack Kellet*

So why, when the journey to Iona and the living conditions in the camps were so apparently unpleasant, did the campers return year after year in droves?

Well, firstly, it exposed the campers to new people and new experiences:

'What the Youth Camps did was to bring together young people, many of them from these working-class areas that now had guys from the Iona Community as ministers. They recommended the thing: "Go on, you'll have a laugh;" and they came, and they had a laugh. They found they were thrown together with people from areas they'd never heard of, and the kind of people that they'd never heard of. It was a totally different experience from anything else they'd ever had in their life.'
– *Walter Fyfe*

'If your mother at home had asked you to peel the spuds, you wouldn't have been very pleased, but you would have to do it. However, we had our potato-peeling duties and vegetable-preparing duties, and we all did it together. All different people, from all different walks of life, all round one big tub, peeling spuds. And the conversation was good. You learned a lot.'
– *Isobel Blair*

'Anybody between 17 and 25 could book in, and it was always a really good mixture of folk. There would be studenty-types, or folk that were at school. There would be folk that were unemployed, or apprentices. It was just a good social mix.'
– *Pat Justad*

It was also, for most campers, their first experience of 'Iona' worship:

'When we arrived, we were given a routine of what our day would be, and I thought, "I'm on holiday here! Why am I going to a morning service first thing?" That didn't seem like a holiday to me! However, up

we got every morning and away to morning service in the Abbey –
which was lovely. And it got, after a few days that, if they'd suddenly
said to you, "There's no morning service this morning," you'd have
been quite lost! It seemed the natural thing to do when you were there.'
– *Isobel Blair*

'We went to every service. And it wasn't a chore – even in the rain. We
put on our rain gear, and we were there for morning service. And if
there was something during the day, we were there, and again in the
evening. And we loved it. I think we were very open. It was the
music. It was the poetry. It was Scottish. And we liked the responsive
worship. It suited our whole feeling of doing things together, of not
just one person standing at the front, doing all that had to be done.
We really liked the participation.'
– *Patsy Colvin*

'Listening to George MacLeod preaching changed my whole life really.
To listen to him preaching in the Abbey, it was the voice of God.'
– *Margaret Hughes*

Even campers who had no background of church attendance or participation in worship were drawn in:

'We arrived at midday on the Saturday, rough and ready, most of us
having never been to church, barely heard of Iona, and were pitched
into this experience where, for instance, we found ourselves the
following morning, Sunday morning, singing our hearts out in a BBC
broadcast, and realising, "Gosh, we can do this thing!" It was different.
There was life. There was vitality. And in the course of that week,
experiencing this extraordinary, very basic, practical, but, at the same
time, strangely spiritual, numinous thing that we hadn't words for. We
were all changed to some extent or other. And that got me hooked.'
– *Jim Hughes*

The Youth Camps were also an opportunity for young people to get
involved in Bible study which was both relevant to their experience and
took the Bible seriously:

'Bible study I didn't look forward to at all. When we got up to the Abbey, we were all divided into groups, and a spokesman would be appointed who had to take notes of what we'd discussed. And at the end of the study, John MacMillan would call for all we had discussed, and what conclusions we'd come to. And, of course, once again, that became a routine, and we all enjoyed it.'
– *Isobel Blair*

'The "See, Judge, Act" method of Bible study was enormously meaningful. It appealed. It had a directness. We were, for 17-, 18-, 19-year-olds, quite socially and politically aware. We had come through the general election [of 1945]. Most of us saw that this was a time for new ways of doing things. And that was why so much of Iona appealed to us. Even at that point, the relevance of the Gospel came through to us, but I think the strands that really got hold of us – the strong things that came through – were worship and service.'
– *Patsy Colvin*

All of this, of course, was testament to the careful preparation of camp leaders like John Jardine:

'There would be a programme of Bible study and discussion, and what we began to develop was a kind of socio-drama way of approaching questions – trying to imagine yourself in other people's shoes. "How would you act in this situation?" Or "Pretend that you are living in an African country …" Or it might be some kind of dispute at a workplace, or it might be a difficult personal relationship. I remember there was one where it started off: "The band is playing 'Temptation'" – I think that was a song at one stage. Anyway, these little settings were established, and, of course, the show-offs really thoroughly enjoyed themselves, and the quiet ones, they came out a wee bit.'
– *John Jardine*

The camp leaders and adult members of the Community also made a huge personal impact on the young campers:

'We were teenagers, and the grown-ups who joined us from the

Community up the hill – from the Abbey – they were grown-ups that were very different from our own parents and the grown-ups at church. They were different in that they were very friendly, and accepting, and jokey with us. People that I know later became quite leading people – like Tom Allan – peeled potatoes with us. And George MacLeod had visitors – philosophers and theologians – and they took a turn of going to the Youth Camps and sharing the chores.'
– *Patsy Colvin*

'We were just little, humble campers. We were nothing. We weren't important. But George MacLeod always came and had a meal in the little hut, and he would sit down, and he would sing all the camp songs, and he would chat to us.'
– *Margaret Hughes*

'It was a great experience. George MacLeod himself undoubtedly had a great influence on me, and so had Ralph Morton and Penry Jones. These people were very important figures. So these were very important days, and that was the beginning of my involvement in the life of the Community.'
– *Stewart McGregor*

It was no accident that the Youth Campers felt this way. The early camp leaders were clear about how they saw their role. For them, it was primarily about relationship:

'I remember the August of 1950, when Penry and Beryl Jones and I led the North End camp. It rained for 28 days, so our first objective was to keep them cheerful. That's where we learned our repartee and our ability to tell jokes, because you had to entertain them after lunch, or after breakfast. You had to get them up at 8am, and walk them to the Abbey by 8.30. They came back, again in the rain, then they had breakfast, and then Bible study, day after day. You had to be tough to do it!'
– *Ian Renton*

'I often say I was a big sister to them in my early days, and then when I got to forty, I began to be a motherly kind of person. And so I began

to think of them as children – as my children.'
– *Alice Scrimgeour*

And at the very heart of the Iona experience was the opportunity to live in community, even if it was just for a week:

'It was such a wonderful, fresh experience. I've a job not to cry think- ing about it. It was just so amazing, the fellowship. I can't put into words what it was, but it was a magic feeling to be part of that Youth Camp group. Quite, quite wonderful.'
– *Margaret Hughes*

'One of the earliest memories I have to do with the Youth Camps was of a Saturday, which was the change-over day. The "King George" came on the Saturday and took the old campers away, and brought the new ones. Even if it was a beautiful day, you wouldn't go away to the beach or anything: you had to be in the village for "steamer-time" – the couple of hours when the boat was in. The bit of grass in front of Iona Cottage was just covered: the old campers sat on this grassy bit and sang, welcoming the new ones in. And the farewells – this is such a part of Iona, the arrivals and the departures – the kind of intense farewells of people who'd got to know each other really well over a week.'
– *Molly Harvey*

But most of all, the camps were great fun:

'The design of the camp programme was specifically to help them to see the integrated nature of the Christian faith, but it was also to give them a good time. There were dances, and swimming parties, and all that stuff. The tents in the North End were bell-tents, old army bell- tents, and they blew down in gales. And we had tremendous fun with that. It was just terrific fun there.'
– *John Harvey*

'Every Friday night there was a dance in the village hall. These were really wonderful Scottish country dances. Real ceilidhs they were! And they didn't really start until 10 or 11 at night.'
– *Margaret Hughes*

'I went to it at 8pm and left after 5am. I always remember that the floor was very rough, and the music was supplied by dubious 78 vinyl records, and a man who played badly on the melodeon. The lighting was from a central paraffin lamp which was suspended from the ceiling. It was a Tilley lamp, and when the lamp fizzled out through lack of pressure, someone came and lowered it down on a rope, and we pumped it up again. And in these days we not only did all the Highland dances and eightsome reels, we did sixteensome reels!'
– *Ian Renton*

It's clear that, for the vast majority of campers, a week on Iona was a life-enhancing and, potentially, life-changing experience. For some, however, the Youth Camps were the means by which they were recruited into the membership of the Community. Stewart McGregor and Jim Hughes are typical examples:

'In 1948, I went with a group of members of my Youth Fellowship to a Youth Camp. That year, the Youth Camp was in the village school, and we lived there with others from other youth groups, and we shared in the worship of the Abbey, and we enjoyed the island. And that was the beginning of my involvement in the life of the Community. After that, I went back to Iona every year for a large number of years, and when I became a student, I used to go up, first as a camper, then as a camp leader. I led the tented camp at the North End, and I also ran a camp in the village until 1957, when I joined the Community.'
– *Stewart McGregor*

'In 1952, my future wife, Margaret, took me up to the Youth Camps. We returned the following year, and that was when the connection really started. My connection was mainly this youth thing – this "Iona experience" – living in the village camp, and doing all the basic chores, and this peculiar thing going on in the Abbey, and encountering George MacLeod and the other members, and realising that there was something here. Not sure what it was, but feeling enthusiastic about it. But mainly, enjoyment: a sense of fun, a sense of vitality, and no relationship to the sombre Presbyterianism of my upbringing, and my West of Scotland guilt. And we found ourselves more and more engaged in this.

I became a Youth Associate – and then in 1958/59 a former university colleague of mine, another engineer, asked me if I had ever considered joining the Community. And I thought, "Well, not really." He said, "Well, Ralph Morton would like to speak to you." So Ralph duly did speak to me, and what Ralph said was quite direct and simple. He said, "What we need in the Community is irritants, and I think lay people are the best irritants. So, basically, will you come in and help us to irritate the Community?" And I fell for this, and joined, and was very pleased to join.'
– *Jim Hughes*

But, of course, not everyone felt called in this way. So what did the leaders hope the average camper would take away with him or her at the end of their week on the island?

'Well, I hoped that they would take away the "Iona" thing. Not to separate religion from life. That you can't have a religious bit to your life: that it's got to spill over, or your life has to spill over into it.'
– *Alice Scrimgeour*

'Well, one of the things would be a happy experience of living in community with other people. It would be that worship could be significant and enjoyable, and that they could take part in it. And a wider view of the world, in terms of the way in which the study programmes dealt with serious matters, important matters.'
– *John Jardine*

'I remember one group that came with a man from Greenock, and somebody asked him: "What do you feel that your young people learn from being here?" And he was brilliant. He just said, "Never considered the question." He said, "I just wanted them to know that they had access to a place like this." And that, I think, was our philosophy: that they had access to a place like this, and could come. And I think that what happens is: that then changes their relationship, and their loyalty, and their solidarity, and their interests. In present-day speak, people don't feel "marginalised": they feel part of a greater whole – a civil society.'
– *Jim Robertson*

But what happened when the young people left Iona?

'When they left Iona, we said, "Come to the reunion in October or November in Community House in Clyde Street." And they all came, with great excitement. And it obviously meant so much to them. They came from all the airts to this reunion, and we had a wonderful time meeting and re-meeting, leaders and campers alike.'
– *Ian Renton*

'Community House offered young people the same meeting-point – again, a place where they would be accepted. Like Iona, there was a sense of wholeness there.'
– *Jim Robertson*

'I was quite active in the Youth Associates – people who came to the Youth Camps often became Youth Associates. We had reunions in Community House, and we shared in the discipline of the Community. It was a way of relating what had happened on Iona to the life of young people on the mainland.'
– *Stewart McGregor*

Although Community House in Glasgow functioned primarily as the mainland headquarters of the Iona Community, it had come about originally as the result of a youth initiative:

'Sir James Lithgow wanted to give some money to Mr Smith who was the minister of Kelvingrove Church – one of the Charing Cross churches in Glasgow – who was also the Convener of the Youth Committee of the Church of Scotland. So he offered it to the Youth Committee to experiment with young people, and the Church of Scotland Youth Committee said that they couldn't experiment. They had to be right! Imagine! They couldn't see themselves putting over something that they were doubtful about! So they refused, and Sir James had to think again. So he made it a united thing between the Church of Scotland and the Iona Community, and it was called the "Iona Youth Trust".'
– *Alice Scrimgeour*

'This was an endeavour, during the war years, to make some sort of impact on serving the youth of the nation, through the life of the Church. This money allowed George MacLeod to do all kinds of innovative things. The first thing he was able to do was to take over a big warehouse, down the Broomielaw,[11] and convert it into a huge community centre. It was not so much a youth centre as the centre of the Iona Community's work during the winter months, but all kinds of activities were taking place there, including activities for young people.'
– *John Sim*

Community House became an important point of contact for the Youth Campers in the months after they left camp. The transition from the high days of their week on Iona to the ordinariness of their everyday lives on the mainland was often a difficult one, as Pat Justad discovered:

'We had terrible withdrawal symptoms when we came back from Iona. We would try and replicate some of the things – maybe had a youth service at the church – to try and bring back some of what we'd had on Iona. But that was always very difficult.'
– *Pat Justad*

It was a problem that the camp leaders were well aware of:

'There's always been the difficulty of translating the Iona experience back to the mainland. It's still there. And you'd always get the difficulties of a lot of young people getting caught by the whole thing, and then going back to a traditional church, and getting very frustrated.'
– *John Harvey*

'When they went back to their church, we got them to promise not to say too much about Iona, but just to get on with being a Christian, because people were a bit unhappy if people came back fanatically Iona-orientated. It tended to put some of them off.'
– *Ian Renton*

Consequently, Community House became the place where young people who were feeling deflated by the transition from the heights of Iona to the toil of everyday life could meet and talk openly about their new-found insights, and learn more about the new worlds that had been opened up to them on Iona:

> 'People did suffer a kind of "burst balloon" when they got back, and I suppose that's when we began to go into Community House quite a lot.'
> – *Isabel Whyte*

> 'It's hard to say actually what gripped me, but Iona was so different from the kind of church that I grew up in, which was a bit dull, and old-fashioned, and well-behaved. But then, sometime in the autumn, there was the Iona Reunion which happened in Community House!
>
> I think we stayed one night or two nights. You could go on Friday and stay until Sunday, if you didn't live in Glasgow. And that was a sort of shortened version of going to Iona: everything was fitted in, but in a weekend. And that got me interested in Community House and what was going on there.'
> – *Marion Jack*

So what was going on in Community House?

The first Wardens of the House were Ralph and Jenny Morton. Their daughter, Faith, remembers the early days of their involvement:

> 'In 1943, when the Iona Youth Trust was formed, and funding had been given for this experimental work with young people, and they were planning to have some sort of Centre in Glasgow, George MacLeod did write and ask my parents to come and be the Wardens of this new Community House. And so they moved up to Glasgow in 1943, taking all the family with them, although, at that stage, they hadn't even got a property.
>
> Community House was an amazing place. Especially if you actually lived there, which we did when eventually they got the building, and got it adapted as they wanted – which was quite a struggle. The whole idea of Community House in Clyde Street was that it should be open to everyone, and there were no doors closing off. So you went into this very large reception area with tables and chairs, and that was the

restaurant, but the kitchen off it was also open. Anybody could look in and see what was happening. There were no walls there, and the same thing with the chapel. There was a little chapel at the back, and every lunchtime there was a short service there, which went on while people were eating their lunches and making conversation. So this was the whole idea: that it was open, accessible to anyone who came in off the street.'
– *Faith Aitken*

'It was designed as an open house. In a way, it was a fine example of a lot of the Community's thinking put into operation. It's important to visualise on the ground floor a big open space with great big windows, like big shop windows, looking out onto Clyde Street, which was a busy street. And all sorts of people came in to eat: office workers, people going to travel on the buses, down-and-outs. People who just wanted to shelter out of the rain came in and sat.'
– *John Jardine*

'I still see it in my mind's eye: you had criminals, borstal boys, Divinity students, students from the university, people off the street in for lunch. Everyone.'
– *Ian Renton*

'There was a bus terminus just on the other side of the street, and the bus crews came in for their break, so that there would always be some of those as well. And the place was open in the evenings too, because they ran classes there. My mother certainly was very closely involved with planning these courses, and looking after the mechanics of how the House ran.

In some summers, when my father was up on Iona, she would stay to keep things going at Community House. Also, in the summer months, they would run a kind of hostel in the upper floors for people who wanted to stay a night in Glasgow on their way to and from Iona.'
– *Faith Aitken*

'We used to sleep in the attic in Community House, because we had to leave for Iona at four o'clock in the morning. It was diabolical when you think about it. There were iron bedsteads with army blankets, and the most appalling plumbing that you have ever heard. The noise in those pipes was deafening. There was a boys' dorm and a girls' dorm, of course. I don't know which one had the worse plumbing.'
– *Isabel Whyte*

'By then, there was quite a staff. The restaurant had Muriel Morton as the manageress, and she had a team of wonderful people under her in the kitchen. There was Oliver Wilkinson who looked after the Drama, and, later on, Penry Jones [Industrial Secretary]. So it needed to have somebody like my mother as a kind of "Co-ordinator in Charge".

We lived upstairs where, again, there was no front door. Anybody could wander into our flat. It was just up another stair from the main building, and in no way shut off.'
– *Faith Aitken*

'The thing about the Wardens' flat was – and many a joke was made about this by guffawing male members of the Community – anybody could walk in the door downstairs and walk right up to Jenny Morton's bedroom! Mind you, if they met Jenny on the way, they wouldn't have gone any further. She was pretty formidable. But she was also very welcoming. You'd go up there, and you got hospitality. They had a big sitting room, and many a party was held up there.'
– *John Jardine*

'So that was very much the philosophy of the whole house, and certainly my maternal grandmother and my aunt did not think this was a suitable place to bring up children. My mother's family were very hostile and suspicious of this whole enterprise. You looked down from the windows of our kitchen to a pub across the road, you know! It certainly wasn't a particularly salubrious part of Glasgow to be in. But I think it was a fascinating education for us children. There were other people coming and going all the time, and you heard them all having meetings. The staff would have their meetings up in our sitting room. There would be discussions, arguments, all kinds of

interesting visitors. So it really was a very stimulating place.'
– *Faith Aitken*

As Faith indicates, at the heart of Community House were a number of classes, aimed primarily at young people:

'There were four main divisions that they were planning to cover. One was "The Faith", as they called it. That was on "What is Christianity?" basically. And then there was "The Faith and Social Order" which was all on politics and economics. There were also, interestingly, courses on film, and courses on drama, because George MacLeod felt those were very important channels of communication. And so people could register for these classes, and they went on for a series. The drama people produced some plays or productions of their own, and all of that was very, very stimulating for youngsters.'
– *Faith Aitken*

Alice Scrimgeour, whose office was in Community House, vividly remembers the drama and film classes:

'Oliver Wilkinson made a play about the Community and what it was doing, and he took it round, outside, on a lorry, and it was very good. Russell Ferguson ran a film class, teaching people about the use of films, and cameras, and things like that. And he made a film of the Community at one stage. He went round Community House filming us all at our work. I met George MacLeod when I went up to the camps, and he said to me, "You're quite photogenic."'
– *Alice Scrimgeour*

Faith Aitken's brother, Colin, also has cause to remember the drama classes:

'Oliver Wilkinson was a lovely character. He was getting people to write their own drama, you know – it was very much community drama – and trying to encourage people in churches to use drama more. And there was also a strong connection with the "Citizens' Theatre"[12] at that time. They were both putting on plays, and going out and doing plays in the city streets. You felt it was dealing with real issues. Oliver was in touch with people who were playing a significant part in British theatre, but I think there were also people in the Citizens' who wanted to link up with the whole community drama aspect of it.

I remember there was one holiday time when I acted as an extra in the Citizens' Theatre. It was *The Merchant of Venice*. It landed up there were two of us who were doing most of the extras. I was very thin at that time, about as tall as I am now [6 foot plus!] and a bit of string, and the other one was a rather short, dumpy person. In *The Merchant of Venice*, you have these three "casket" scenes – that went fine, except when they had a school matinee. The whole Citizens' Theatre was packed with school children. So, first time, we went in and drew the curtains back. Second time, loud cheers when we came on! Third time, we'd to stop the play for a bit, which was quite embarrassing, you know! And these good actors had to wait until we took our bows.'
– *Colin Morton*

For others, it was the classes run by Penry Jones that made the greatest impact:

'Penry Jones was Industrial Secretary, and used to run conferences for people in industry. And I think it had a general effect on the whole of Scotland, not just in the Church, but in aspects of industry.'
– *Ian Renton*

'Penry Jones was my political mentor. I've always felt that the only way to really make change is in Westminster. You could, maybe, be a protest group, but Penry said, "That's not enough!"'
– *Peggy Bee*

'There was a period of time in Scotland when many of the opinion-makers in Scottish society were people who had cut their teeth in Community House. Jimmy Reid was a good example. He was one of the leaders of the Apprentices' Strike. George Thomson, for example, was quite prominent. He joined the Labour Party, and was editor of *Forward*, the Labour newspaper, and I remember him using people from the Iona Community, including myself, to write articles for it. He became an MP and went into Harold Wilson's

cabinet – he was Commonwealth Secretary – and later on joined the European Commission.'
– *Walter Fyfe*

News of the exciting things that were going on at Community House spread well beyond Glasgow. As a young person, Molly Harvey longed to be part of it:

'We lived first of all in Leith, and then in Dundee, and after having been on Iona and met some of these people, I remember thinking that Glasgow must be the most exciting place to be, because people talked about Community House in Glasgow, and all the things that were going on there. And I remember, as a teenager, thinking, "Oh God, I wish I lived in Glasgow!" Because here were we going back to the east coast, where it seemed so unrelated and unexciting! And I can remember driving with the family back from some place, and coming into Glasgow at one point, and thinking, "Oh, I might see a member of the Iona Community in the street!" That's the kind of feeling it had.'
– *Molly Harvey*

Later, in the 1960s, Douglas Alexander became Warden of Community House, but he had encountered it first as a child:

'I was a ten-year-old schoolboy, and my father, who was a Church of Scotland minister in Eaglesham, had brought me into Glasgow. The [bus] terminus was in Clyde Street, and my father brought me off the bus, and said, "I want you to see somewhere interesting," and he took me across the road, literally, to 214 Clyde Street – Community House. I'm talking about the year 1945/46. And having taken me into Community House, we sat on the window seat – I can see it clearly – and the people were all milling around the restaurant, as was the fashion. And this very tall, distinguished-looking guy walked through the restaurant, and my father said to me, "Look, that's George MacLeod. He's a minister in our Church, and a very important person."'
– *Douglas Alexander*

But by the time Douglas became Warden of Community House in the early 1960s, there was a feeling that its glory days had gone:

'When I was appointed at the very beginning of the 1960s, everybody tended to look back to the golden years of Community House as being the end of the '40s, after the war, when people had come back and flooded into the House for "classes", as they were called, in "film-making", in "political discussion", in all kinds of creative arts. The '50s had seen the House peak, and begin to come down, in the sense of having slightly lost its way. It was no longer sure of quite what its role was, and that was fairly openly admitted by everybody involved. So when I did take over in the early '60s, I knew that the House had to rediscover a role for itself. And I can remember the key words of the time: we set out to be "A centre for meeting, for sharing, for studying, and serving", and using these as headline words, we developed a whole programme over the years of the '60s.

A major endeavour during the '60s was to try and explore what subsequently became known as "urban mission". That term was not being used in the early '60s, but Community House was one of the pioneers in Britain of urban ministry, or urban mission. We tried to draw together the insights of the Christian faith and the insights and experience of those who were involved in running the systems of society: I mean town planners, sociologists, doctors – people who made the city the kind of place that it was. We tried to bring those groups together and, to a very remarkable degree, we succeeded, and it was a very exciting and dynamic phase. To see the release that people found when they came for interdisciplinary seminars under the heading of "Rebuilding the City"! And, of course, at that time Glasgow was undergoing massive rehabilitation. It was the age of the tower blocks rising, and from the door of Community House, one could see the great flats of Basil Spence[13] just across the river, which, of course, twenty years or so later, all had to be demolished, because it was a disaster. But all of that was part of the study, and the talk, and the converse of Community House.'
– *Douglas Alexander*

And in the midst of all this 'study, and talk, and converse', the House's commitment to young people never wavered:

'Many, many young people particularly enjoyed coming into Community House. During the '60s, we routinely would have four occasions in the winter when we would have up to four hundred young people garnered from the Youth Fellowships. We had a very carefully worked-out programme whereby they came into Community House, let's say it was around seven o'clock, and we had them for two-and-a-half hours. And the evening consisted of moving them round the different areas of the House. I don't mean just the physical areas, but the different sectors of the House's involvement with politics, with industry, with worship, with alcoholism, gambling and whatever. We exposed those youngsters to the whole nature of Community House, and many, many of them became firm friends of the Iona Community, and ended up going to the island to find out more.'
– *Douglas Alexander*

In a sense, Community House was maturing along with the Iona Community. The Church of Scotland, for instance, seems to have adopted a more relaxed attitude to its activities during the 1960s:

'If I can be "George MacLeodian", and be outrageously terse: the Church of Scotland's view of Community House in the 1940s? Hostility! In the 1950s? A pretty strong suspicion. In the 1960s? A more tolerant resignation – letting that Iona bunch do their thing, because by then the Iona bunch had demonstrated that they knew what they were on about. So, from hostility, through suspicion, to a kind of resigned toleration, and, latterly, a grudging respect.'
– *Douglas Alexander*

And, interestingly, when pushed to identify the centrally important feature of Community House during the 1960s, Douglas Alexander comes up with the answer which the very first Wardens, Ralph and Jenny Morton, would probably have given:

'Its genius was in providing a context where people who would not normally come into contact with each other did come into contact. A complete mixture of disciplines, and a complete mixture of people searching to clarify what discipleship means in contemporary terms.'
– *Douglas Alexander*

Indeed, this was the genius of Community House, and it always had been, as Faith Aitken illustrates with a story from the 1940s:

'There were all sorts of characters around Community House, as you can imagine, including various borstal boys. George MacLeod was very involved with Polmont Borstal in those days, and used to bring some of the boys up to Camas [the Community's Adventure Centre on Mull], and some of them appeared at Community House afterwards. I particularly remember one boy – large and solid – who was hanging around Community House at the time when I was just starting college in Cambridge. And at the end of my first term at Newnham, at this residential, girls-only college, I was shattered, one evening, to rush into my room and find this boy sitting there in my bed-sitting room in the large wellington boots which he always seemed to wear. And he just announced that he knew the end of my term was coming, and he had come to take me home. I was horrified, and didn't know what any of my friends, let alone the authorities, would think, because there were all kinds of strict rules about when you had men in the college at all. And so, I had a very difficult time over the next few days, trying to hide the fact that he was there. And he did escort me all the way back to Glasgow! I only discovered afterwards that he had taken money from the till at Community House in order to finance this trip to Cambridge!'
– *Faith Aitken*

In telling her story of the boy, Faith refers to George MacLeod's involvement with Polmont Borstal, and to the Community's Adventure Centre at Camas on Mull. And, indeed, it would be impossible to tell the story of the Community's youth work without telling the story of Camas and the 'Borstal Boys'.

As a student, Douglas Trotter accompanied the first members of the Iona Community to the island in 1938. He found himself doing very ordinary chores for the Community, but there is one task which he still remembers vividly:

'During my first year or two on Iona, I wasn't a full member of the Community. I did a lot of scrubbing floors, and things like that, in the

"Rome Express". But one particular project I got was Camas. The Community rented little fishermen's cottages at Camas. They were for salmon fishing, and the method of fishing was to stretch nets across the mouth of the little outlet into the sea. As you can imagine, it was in a bit of a mess after the fishermen, but we scrubbed it, and then we made it possible for two or three people to come and stay there.'
– *Douglas Trotter*

Conditions at Camas made the 'Rome Express' look like a luxury hotel:

'Camas was a row of granite, double-storeyed houses – a terrace, really, of maybe five dwellings, originally quarry workers' houses, later used as a salmon-fishing station. And then there was also a row of unroofed, single-storey cottages which were just an empty, derelict ruin, although the walls were there. Of the double-storey ones, the Community had one lower house, but then, upstairs, you could walk right along the whole top floor, as it were. All the water had to be carried from wells. There was no running water whatsoever. And there was, of course, no electricity.'
– *John Jardine*

So why would George MacLeod want to acquire a derelict salmon-fishing station? Hadn't he taken on quite enough when he set out to restore the Abbey?

'I think George was very keen that we should resurrect the salmon fishing for the same reasons that we [were keen to] farm on Iona. Cosmic redemption! You've got to do everything. Anyway, he got a fisherman over from Peterhead called Charles Forman, and Charlie Forman was charged with showing us how to start fishing. I can remember that one of the first things we did, just to show there was fish around, and that we could get them, was to fish for haddock off the shore of Iona, off Martyrs' Bay. We would dig up worms, and then we would string them on long lines – oh, two hundred on each line – and we caught fish!'
– *Douglas Trotter*

George MacLeod's daughter, Mary, remembers how she felt about Camas, as a child:

'What I thought was really exciting about Camas was that it was a salmon-fishing station, and my father had to be registered as a fishmonger in order to sell the salmon. I thought that was much more interesting than him being a minister, or him being the Leader of the Iona Community. To have your father as a fishmonger seemed to be just so exciting.'
– *Mary MacLeod*

At first, the small groups of senior school boys and theological students who came to stay at Camas seem to have found it equally exciting:

'We had to, of course, make our own lives there. We climbed Ben More. We went to the Friday night dance in Bunessan,[14] and came across the moor at four or five in the morning, trudging all the way from Bunessan back to Camas. We sometimes slept out on the hill in the heather. Took our blankets up, and it was lovely, soft and springy. To waken up with the sun rising – marvellous! We went over to "Traigh na Margaidh" – Market Bay – and swam there. So these were heady days. It was a good time.'
– *Stewart McGregor*

'We used to go up the hills round about. There must have been about six of us. Now, we were all theological students, and we were all supposed to be committed to each other and to the right way of living, so we said, in our stupidity and our ignorance, "Och well, we'll all just work in together and share the chores." We'd no rota. Now, it was just a mess. It didn't work. We stayed up too late at night – we liked sitting with an open fire – and eventually one fellow just fled. Disappeared. So we were going all over the place, shouting, looking for him, and we couldn't find him, and we really got very, very worried. Eventually, after many hours, he came back, and he said, "I was just so tired, I went away and I fell asleep." He'd been sleeping away out on a hill somewhere, in beautiful weather, and once he'd had his sleep, he came back, and he was all right. Our life was very undisciplined!'
– *John Jardine*

In time, however, George MacLeod developed a wider vision for Camas that placed it firmly in the tradition of the Christian Workers' League.

John Jardine was among the group of Youth Camp leaders who would go up to Iona at the start of the season, to prepare for the summer ahead:

> 'After we'd set up the North End camp, we went over to Camas and we worked there. Charlie Kirkpatrick took us over in his boat. We took over supplies, and blankets, and all sorts of stuff like that, and got Camas organised over a period of time. Eventually, it was going to be used for a group of borstal boys. There was also a local salmon fisherman called Alan MacInnes, and, for the salmon-fishing season, he came with his daughter, Annie, who would be in her teens.'
> – *John Jardine*

Annie Macrae was just 19 when she, her sister, Katie, and her father, Alan, took over the fishing at Camas from Charlie Forman:

> 'My father had lost the fishing in Carsaig,[15] and he had nowhere to fish then, and somebody suggested he go and ask Dr George [MacLeod]. So he went away to Iona, and came back all smiles, because he got the Camas fishing. They had a man before us who came from Aberdeen, and he had a different way of fishing, and he had these huge heavy nets that us two girls couldn't lift, with my father on the end and us two at the other. They were useless to us – big brutes of things – so they were left in the "Chapel of the Nets" up the outside stairs in Camas.'
> – *Annie Macrae (née MacInnes)*

The 'Chapel of the Nets' was created by Douglas Trotter and Colin Day, in preparation for the arrival of the 'Borstal Boys':

> 'We extended the sleeping accommodation into a little hostel. And one thing I remember, vividly, is designing and building what has come to be called the "Chapel of the Nets" in which everything – the seats and the Communion table – is part of the fishing equipment.'
> – *Douglas Trotter*

'The "Chapel of the Nets", at that time, had lots of nets hanging down from the rafters, and then a middle place where there was wee black barrels, and you sat on a black barrel. There was more nets on the stances, and there was a ship's rudder, and that held the Bible. There was a table with two big barrels and good boards across there, and that was covered again with one layer of net. And they had old bits – a block and tackle – well, the tackle was out of it – it was just the iron framework – and the candles on the table. It was really very nice. They weren't long services. We would read a bit, and then we would sing a bit. Oh, we had some nice services up there.'
– *Annie Macrae (née MacInnes)*

The relationship established between the Community and the MacInnes family seems to have been close and creative:

'Alan was a delightful gentleman. We got on fine with him, as long as we didn't do anything stupid, like interfere with his nets or any of his equipment, which we were much too wise to do. They went out twice a day with two nets, and opened them up at the weekends, because you weren't allowed to catch salmon on a Sunday. They opened them on a Saturday night, so that the salmon couldn't get caught, and they went away back to Carsaig, and returned on the Monday morning. But otherwise they stayed in one of the lower houses of the terrace.'
– *John Jardine*

'At night, while I was away for the milk, Dr George would come in, and Dad and him would put the world to rights. When I would come home, they would be there, going at it "good-o". He was really a very entertaining man right enough. He'd been in the Great War like Dad had, so they had things to talk about.

It must have been May before the first lot of borstal boys came to Camas – there was quite a group of them, and then there was two or three warders with them, and there was Community folk, and Dr George as well. Dr George's idea was that it would do them the world of good to come and see how other folk lived, because they were mostly from the bad ends of Glasgow and Edinburgh.'
– *Annie Macrae (née MacInnes)*

'Over the years, the Community had established links with one borstal in particular – what's now called "Polmont Young Offenders' Institution", I think, but known as a borstal in those days.

The "Borstal Boys" would be probably 16-18 years old, that kind of age group. They would come with their prison officers. They were already under quite a high degree of discipline within the institution, so they were actually some of the easiest groups to work with, in the sense that, for them, this was a huge privilege to be allowed to come for a week to Camas, and if they stepped out of line for a minute, they might well end up back in the institution again. So, in that sense, there was quite a lot of pressure on them to behave, if they really wanted to complete their experience. But, like Iona, their contact with other young people, and with some of the leaders, was often of huge importance to them, because, again, it was an opportunity to meet young people from a different social background, with different ideas, and to have time to talk some of those ideas through. And just to see a different world from the one that they were used to.'
– *Tor Justad*

'One of the plans they had hatching was that we would take a couple of boys out every day. But the boat wasn't very big, and some of them liked it, and some of them didn't, so it gradually fell off. But they were very good if you wanted a hand with lifting the nets up a bit. They would almost all do it. They were good, the borstal boys: they helped us quite a lot. They were on their best behaviour. And one night a week they would take them to Iona to a dance or something.

There was an old chap – Johnny MacMillan – and he and Tom Colvin, they came from Iona nearly every day when the borstal boys were there, with supplies, and to see how things were going on. And they were nice people too: we got to know them very well. The leaders sometimes had us in for a meal at night. They had a coal-burning or wood-burning stove, and they had a gas stove, and it was done out as a kitchen, and a hatchway through to their dining area. Then they had a big room next to that, facing down to the sea, and it had a good fireplace in it, and that was where they would gather at night,

especially if it was pouring rain, and have their sing-songs, and whatever stories they had then.'
– *Annie Macrae (née MacInnes)*

The MacInnes family seem to have had genuine affection for both George
MacLeod and the borstal boys – as well as a large dose of patience:

'Dr George would get in bed, and the boys would have a smelly old
fish – mackerel or something – hanging, and they would lower it
down and torment him. So up he would get then, roaring around, and
cowping them all out of their beds. And we didn't get any sleep either,
because it was just one layer of flooring. There wasn't two layers of
flooring to deaden the sound. He was a great case!

And then he would have them up early, and out: "Out for a swim! Out
for a swim!" Well, he didn't get very many to go with him, but one or
two would be coaxed into doing this, and he would swim away out,
and he would swim back in. I mean, he was quite an old man then.
He used to say to us: "You should come!" But I can't swim. None of us
could swim. I often think what a chance we took, because none of us
could swim.'
– *Annie Macrae (née MacInnes)*

In the late 1960s, the Community's links with Polmont Borstal took on a
new dimension with the creation of the 'Six Circle Group':

'In addition to Camas, on Iona there was an annual group which was
known as the "Six Circle Group". It had been formed and inspired by
a governor at Polmont Borstal called Charlie Hills, who was an
Englishman who had worked in the prison service in Scotland for
many years. He hit on the idea of looking for a way in which these
borstal lads who, both from their own perspective and society's
perspective, had only "taken" from society – in the sense that they'd
been involved in theft, or crimes of various kinds – could contribute
something back to society, over a short, intensive period. Which
might, in turn, lead them to think they might want to choose that way
in the future.

His idea was to bring together a whole lot of different groups, but the mix, essentially, was between people with disabilities and people who were able-bodied – and to see what that interaction would lead to, and how, in particular, these borstal boys would respond when faced with that situation.

So, each year, they would invite various institutions for the disabled, and various schools and other organisations to take part in this camp. So, typically, you might have four or five different groups, one or more of which were groups of disabled young people, and they would bring their own adult leaders. And the idea was, I think, completely inspirational, and although it's probably quite commonplace these days, in those days it was quite new and innovative.

I can remember, in particular, one occasion which was the weekly pilgrimage around the island, where we had, in this particular group, several young people in wheelchairs and a borstal group. The pilgrimage is an all-day walk around the island, going right down to sea-level to the marble quarry, and right up to the highest point on the island, Dun I, which is somewhere over three hundred feet, and quite a steep climb. And these borstal lads took these wheelchair-bound young people the whole distance of that pilgrimage. On sections where they could push them across the machair,[16] it was relatively straightforward, but imagine wheelchairs being bodily carried down into the marble quarry, back up to the highest point on the island – literally, physically being carried, and these boys busting their guts, basically, to do this, and succeeding at the end of it. It was just inspirational! For everybody watching it, but obviously in particular for the young people themselves – both the ones who were doing the carrying, and the ones in the wheelchairs. And that one picture of those wheelchairs being carried around the island, for me, was proof enough that this theory which this particular governor had was of value – and of lasting value, in many cases.'

– *Tor Justad*

And it's because of experiences like this one that former Iona Community youth worker Jim Robertson is convinced of the importance of the work that was done with young people on Iona, at Camas and in Community House:

> 'We've met borstal boys who bring their partners, years on, to Iona. Not because of the holy bits, or the music stuff. It's because of a sense that they had of identity with it. But hundreds of people felt the same about Community House in Glasgow. It wasn't just to do with Iona – that was quite clear. We tried to generate this sense of being able to go to a place that you weren't marginalised, and be part of the way that it worked. And I don't think that's been repeated anywhere in my experience.'
> *– Jim Robertson*

And so, despite the fact that young people did not figure in George MacLeod's original vision for the Iona Community, perhaps the most significant legacy of the early members has been their contribution to the philosophy and practice of youth work – and to the lives of countless young people who first learned, at their hands, what it meant to 'belong'.

1

4

5

8

9

in 1939, he had 'no connection with the islanders at all', and some who did, later came to realise that, under the surface, all was not well. George Wilkie spent a lot of time in the homes of islanders:

> 'I think that the relationship was not all that good. Although outwardly friendly – and I only came to realise this afterwards when I got to know the islanders – there were all sorts of underlying streams of feeling about the Iona Community.'
> – *George Wilkie*

If George MacLeod had hoped that he would win over the islanders easily, he must have been disappointed. Not only was there continuing suspicion, there was outright opposition. MacLeod certainly seems to have felt the need to constantly explain the Community to the islanders. Ursula MacLeod was a cook at the Abbey for a number of years:

> 'George used to go round the island every summer. He would visit every croft, trying to keep things going.'
> – *Ursula MacLeod*

And such visits weren't confined to the summertime, when the rebuilding of the Abbey was in full swing. George Wilkie accompanied George MacLeod to Iona during the winter of 1947:

> 'George MacLeod wanted to get round the island. I went to one or two houses with him, where he wanted to meet the people, talk with them, and try and overcome this resistance. He did do a lot of that. I think that they were glad to see him, and they thought he was a great guy, but they were very suspicious of what he was after. And, of course, he didn't change his ways in any respect.'
> – *George Wilkie*

So why did the strategy of visitation which had proved so successful in MacLeod's Govan parish, and was later to prove so again in many of the Community's mainland parishes, fail so spectacularly on Iona? George Wilkie's contribution may provide a significant clue: George MacLeod 'didn't change his ways in any respect'. He may have been on a mission to explain, but not, it appears, to listen.

MacLeod's ability to gain the trust of the islanders was, inevitably, limited by his own background and personal style. Joan Low, a girls' leader in the Youth Camps, had the opportunity to observe him at close quarters:

'He was very patrician, it seemed to me, and he walked around like the Laird, which must have irritated a lot of people, because he was an incomer. And he was a powerful man. So I think, from that point of view, people wouldn't necessarily warm to him. I suppose, in one sense, he was always the "officer" and the other people were the "men". And you couldn't get away from that. He just was different.'
– *Joan Low*

Kathy Galloway, a former Leader of the Community, came to the same conclusion:

'I think that a lot of the difficulties related to the way that George did things, actually. George was just high-handed. He was high-handed in the Community. He was high-handed on Iona. I think some of that was unconscious, upper-class, born-to-rule stuff. Clearly, some things could have been more thoughtfully done, but I'm not quite sure how, given who he was.'
– *Kathy Galloway*

The island too was a highly stratified society, and it didn't escape the notice of the islanders that George MacLeod seemed to be more friendly with those at the top of the island hierarchy. Davie Kirkpatrick, whose parents were both employed by the Community at different times, noticed it, even as a child:

'George MacLeod was friendly with the MacPhails at Block House, and the MacPhails, to a certain degree, controlled things at that point in time, because they were the Post Office. They were the hub. They saw everything that came off the ferry or onto the ferry. And the doctor consulted in there in those days. There would only be two or three phones on Iona at that time, so the telegram was a very important thing. And they had the [news] papers, and they had the bread. And George MacLeod, if he came off the ferry, that's where he

went. He didn't go into Seaview to see my father, or my mother, or my granny. It was Block House he went to.'
– *Davie Kirkpatrick*

The contention that the continuing strained relationship between islanders and Community contained a 'class' element appears to be supported by the fact that none of the craftsmen reported any difficulty in their relationships with the islanders. They seem to have been much more readily accepted.

Hugh Lamont and his father both worked on the Abbey:

'It was always a very agreeable association between the permanent craftsmen and the rest of the island. As far as my own experience is concerned, there was nothing that one could look on as a problem. There may have been people on the island who perhaps didn't – "approve" maybe is too strong a word – but I think there may have been some feelings that weren't quite in agreement with Dr MacLeod, or the Abbey, or the Iona Community, but it certainly never affected us, or our relationship with the islanders in any way. That was always excellent.'
– *Hugh Lamont*

It's tempting to suggest that Hugh and other craftsmen who were born and brought up on Mull were more readily accepted, because they were 'locals', and that the young ministers, being drawn mainly from the Central Belt of Scotland, were more likely to be seen as 'outsiders'. Hugh, however, refutes that suggestion:

'To people in Bunessan, Iona was almost another planet. It was miles away. Iona was of no interest – absolutely none. As far as the kids in Bunessan were concerned, it was on the other side of the world. We never went there.'
– *Hugh Lamont*

In addition, craftsmen who came from other parts of Scotland, appear to have formed just as firm friendships with the islanders as the men from Mull did.

John Young was an apprentice joiner from Ayrshire who was recruited by his joinery teacher, Jimmy Bowman, to work on the Abbey during the war:

'We were visiting a croft just up the road from the Abbey. It was two old ladies who lived in it. They had a horse called Charlie, and they had a faulty pump on the outside of the house, where they got their water supply from. It kept breaking down because it was worn, and I don't think they could get replacements for it, but I found that if you reprimed it, you could get it to go – for a short period anyway. So I was up there once or twice, and one of the times when I was up, the horse had been looking for greener grass through the fence, and it had stuck its foot through the fence, and got stuck. I was used to horses actually, so I managed to get the foot out the fence. So, occasionally, later on, I would get a message, "Charlie's put his foot in the fence again," so I went up.

And there was another occasion when a lady down in the village put a lamp too close to a wardrobe, and it charred the surface of the wood. And I don't know why they thought maybe I could fix it, but I managed to fix it. I think I made a cabinet scraper to do it with, and scraped off the stuff, and suggested that they just used Mansion Polish or something, to fill it up. So I think I began to be looked at as "Mr Fix-it", although I was only fifteen years old.'
– *John Young*

It is difficult, in the light of such testimony, to escape the conclusion that there was a 'class' element to the suspicion with which the people of Iona regarded the Community, and that George MacLeod's personal style was indeed a stumbling-block to good relationships in the early days.

Davie Kirkpatrick, however, who still lives on Iona, is surprisingly generous in his assessment of George MacLeod and the early Community:

'George MacLeod did it his way, and I don't think he could have done it any differently. Because you've got to remember, it was just after the war, and people were used to, "Line up there!" and "Go and do this!" and "Go and do that". "Sit at that desk, or you'll get six of the belt." I don't know whether that's right or whether that's wrong, but that's the

way it was at that point in time. So if [the Community] was going to happen on Iona, I don't think they could have done it any differently, because you would have had to call meetings, and meetings were not any different then from what they are today. It would just have been, "Oh, I'll sort that out tomorrow."'
– *Davie Kirkpatrick*

Davie's generosity of spirit suggests that good work has been done by the Community in the years since to repair the damage that was done in the early years. But the Community of today has one huge advantage which the early Community did not. It is not the subject of a concerted dirty tricks campaign by the Scottish media.

There was a great deal of negative coverage of the young Community in the newspapers of the day, and there is no doubt that this coloured the attitudes of the islanders:

'There was a lot of to-ing and fro-ing in the newspapers – the *Glasgow Herald* in particular. The papers were responsible for a lot of chat, rumours, and things that just weren't right at all.'
– *Bill Cooper*

There were three main areas of speculation: the Community was crypto-Catholic; the Community was crypto-Communist; the Community was a hotbed of homosexuality.

Joyce Alexander, who first got to know the islanders in the 1950s through the Youth Camps, felt the effect of these rumours:

'There was antipathy, and there was a feeling of being kept at arm's length. I mean, if the *Daily Record* wrote articles which said the Community was either going to Rome, or it was becoming Communist, or, "What are all these young men doing together?" in those days, as an islander, you would believe that. If you knew what the press was saying about the Community, you would be wary.'
– *Joyce Alexander*

And it wasn't just the islanders who were affected by these stories: people who holidayed on Iona, and even prospective members, like John Jardine, were suspicious at first:

> 'I didn't know much about the Community before I went to Iona, but I used to hear stories about it: there were monks dressed in blue robes going around – that kind of story. I had a friend that used to go to Iona on holiday with his family when he was a boy in the 1930s, and he had stories about the Iona Community which were not altogether flattering.'
> – *John Jardine*

In an age when the general public placed much more trust in the media than they do nowadays, it was difficult for the Community to counter these stories, particularly when their relationship with the local Church of Scotland was so problematic:

> 'The fact of the Abbey being brought to life again, and having worship every Sunday, caused a tension between the Community and the island church – the local church.'
> – *Raymond Bailey*

Given the strong emphasis that the Kirk placed, at that time, on the geographical boundaries of the parish, the fact that George MacLeod was moving into another minister's parish meant that some kind of difficulty was inevitable:

> 'Probably the sense that the whole of Iona was a parish of the Church of Scotland, and here was somebody coming and interfering with that, was one of the points of roughness between the local community, or, at least, the local church community and the Iona Community.'
> – *Ian Fraser*

The problem was exacerbated by the fact that the minister of Iona in those days was nothing like George MacLeod:

> 'There was a minister there who didn't come near George MacLeod's view of ministry and churchmanship, and he was obviously opposed.
> – *George Wilkie*

Flora Brill, although not an islander herself, had strong family ties with
Iona:

'I was married on Iona, and the Iona minister married us – Murdo
Macrae. And he was very, very anti-George MacLeod, because people
would come and say: "Oh, is it not Dr MacLeod preaching?" You
know? The Community, more or less, took over the Abbey, and we
resented it.'
– *Flora Brill*

The early members themselves concede that they could have handled
things better. George Charlton held George MacLeod in the highest
regard, but acknowledges that he was not the kind of minister the
islanders would have chosen:

'Ministers get a feeling that "this is my patch", you know? And I
think, sometimes, we weren't very careful about that kind of thing.
The parish minister just had to put up with the Community in a way.'
– *George Charlton*

Davie Kirkpatrick agrees. He describes the local minister's relationship
with George MacLeod and the Community during the early 1950s as
'strained':

'I think "strained", because – again, it goes back to George MacLeod's
"steamrollering". He proclaimed himself a pacifist, and that maybe is
true regarding weapons of destruction, but his physical presence and
his tongue could do as good a job as a weapon.

Ewen MacLean was the parish minister at that time. He was very
friendly with my father, but I don't know if he got on very well with
the Iona Community. There certainly was no sharing of services the
way there is today. And then Ewen MacLean left, round about the
middle-1950s, and David Stiven came, and David Stiven was the first
minister of Iona that didn't have to have Gaelic, because they were
having a job finding somebody to take the Parish of Iona.'
– *Davie Kirkpatrick*

With the arrival of Dr Stiven, tensions seem to have eased. On a Sunday morning, members of the Community were encouraged to attend both the Community service and the local church service, but still, much of church life seems to have happened in parallel. Ian Mackenzie, however, who was Abbey musician for a time in the 1950s, seems to have managed to straddle both worlds:

> 'On a Sunday, the big Iona Community Communion Service at ten o'clock was utterly inspirational. And then, at twelve, there was the island service – at which I suddenly became the organist for the island, and played the harmonium up by the west door. And I think there were serious efforts by the Community to get people to actually go to that service as well. It never felt right for such a small island to have these two things separate.'
> – *Ian Mackenzie*

And others share Ian's regret:

> 'On the whole, [the islanders] didn't come to the Community services, and it seemed ridiculous that there was a church there with a whole establishment, and the Community. That seemed one of these things that was very, very hard to accept. You could see how George MacLeod wasn't necessarily the kind of minister they would have wanted. But it was a pity. It was sad.'
> – *Joan Low*

Joan, like many others, assumes that the solution would have been for the islanders to give up their service in favour of the Community's. Walter Fyfe, who joined the Community in the 1950s, is well aware that this was unlikely to happen, given that the islanders already felt swamped by the arrival of the Community:

> 'They had their parish church here, and then there's this big alternative up there, and all these people coming who ignore the islanders – who've got nothing to do with them.'
> – *Walter Fyfe*

It would truly have been a remarkable thing if the islanders had allowed their services to be subsumed into the Community's, particularly as their cultural form of Christianity was so different from the Community's.

'We went around visiting each croft, two by two, and it was interest-ing to hear what their reactions were. I can always remember one thing that one said – that there they were, up at the Abbey, and the clothes were hanging out on the clothes lines on the Sunday. And that wasn't nice. Not in the Western Highlands anyway.'
– *Bill Cooper*

'You've got to remember that, at that time, people used to say, "I put my washing out on a Sunday!" as if, "Don't tell anybody!" But the Community just put their washing out, and, of course, that offended some people.'
– *George Wilkie*

Later, George MacLeod would tell, with great glee, the story of how a benefactress had given the Community thousands of pounds, precisely because they had hung out their washing on a Sunday. But, on the whole, MacLeod did try not to flout the conventions of the particular cultural form of Christianity practised by the islanders, of which Sabbath obser-vance was an integral part:

'I got into trouble on one occasion with George MacLeod. A boat came in with some fishermen on board. They had been at sea for three weeks, and they'd never been able to get any exercise, and it was a Sunday. When we learned this, a few of us got together, and we had a game of football up on the Iona stadium.

As soon as I got back that night, George collared me, and said, was I one of those who was playing? He knew well enough already I was one of those who had been playing football on a Sunday, and I knew very well what the islanders would think about this. And I said, "Yes I was, and not only that, these men, for the sake of their health, needed to have a game of football on Sunday, because they'd been at sea for three weeks."

Well, he wasn't very convinced. And I said, "Not only that, Murdo

Ewen Macdonald, preaching in St George's West, said that a new generation of martyrs is needed in the Highlands, and the Iona Community
should be those martyrs." Anyway, George wasn't persuaded. But he
was right to raise that issue: there was tension. But actually it was a
tradition which had somehow to be broken. We had to respect the
islanders, but we had to find, perhaps, other ways of working.'
– *Graeme Brown*

Graeme Brown touches here on the real heart of the dilemma which the
Community faced in relation to the church on the island. Quite often,
they were trying not to offend the sensibilities of the local people, while,
at the same time, offering legitimate challenges to their long-held
preconceptions:

'The Community was a radical movement in those days, and treated
with a lot of suspicion by the Church on the mainland, never mind
the Church on Iona. Most of the islanders rarely darkened the door of
the church, but, nevertheless, would take the side of the church over
against a radical movement like the Community.'
– *Joyce Alexander*

Bill Amos, son of the first master mason to work on the Abbey, has no
doubt that the radical nature of the Community was a major factor in the
islanders' response to them:

'It was the Community's ethics that upset the islanders. George
MacLeod was part of the establishment in a lot of ways – otherwise he
wouldn't have got the money to rebuild the Abbey buildings – but he
was a radical person, and he was a freethinker, and that's the kind of
person that, basically, is going to cause an upset in any society. It
wasn't "Church of Scotland" or whatever the islanders knew about.
It was something completely different. I suppose it's almost like the
Americans coming across here in the Second World War and swamp-
ing the local populace. I think that's what they were frightened of.
And quite right, because the Community did make a difference.'
– *Bill Amos*

Certainly, the Community's bias towards the poor and the marginalised caused difficulty right from the start.

Beryl Jones, whose husband, Penry, was deeply involved in the Community's political and industrial work, recalls the event that tipped the islanders into outright opposition: the arrival of young inmates from Polmont Borstal:

> 'When George dared to bring in the borstal boys, that was the last straw. They didn't stay on the island, they stayed at Camas [the Community's Adventure Centre on Mull], but they were brought over every Sunday for the services. It was just the fact that George had the nerve to bring "these people" here, you know?'
> – *Beryl Jones*

Certainly, part of the islanders' opposition was based on a fear that the presence of young offenders would drive away the kind of wealthy tourist who had, up till then, been crucial to the island's economy. But the sudden arrival of groups of young offenders on a very small island also created a very real fear of crime.

Flora Brill, who spent each summer on the island with her family, remembers how they felt:

> 'George MacLeod decided to invite some borstal boys, and we had to start locking our door at night.'
> – *Flora Brill*

And, to some extent, the islanders' fears were justified. Annie Macrae, whose family were salmon-fishers at Camas at that time, was very supportive of what the Community was trying to do with the boys from Polmont Borstal, but even she has to admit that their leaders had to regularly empty the boys' pockets, and return the pilfered goods they found there to the local shop:

> 'Of course, all their ill-gotten gains went back to where they had come from, but still there were people against having these folk on Iona, a lot of people against them.'
> – *Annie Macrae (née MacInnes)*

So was the Community guilty of naivety – even incompetence – in its early attempts to work with young offenders? It's difficult now to judge. But what is beyond question is that it was guilty of poor communication.

Molly Harvey understands the islanders' anger:

> 'There was a lot of genuine resentment, and I think there was proba-
> bly a lot of very bad practice by all of us who've lived and worked on
> behalf of the Community on the island, in terms of not realising that
> we were treading on people's toes, not taking people along with us.'
> – *Molly Harvey*

Molly may well be right to identify bad practice on the part of the Community, but it is also true that the nature of island life itself made it very difficult for any incomer to form close relationships with islanders.

As a small, isolated community, fearful of losing its identity, Iona resisted new people and new ideas:

> 'I think it is very often exaggerated, to be honest, these so-called
> tensions between the island community and the Iona Community.
> That's not to say that there wasn't a tension: there was. But it wasn't
> really so much because of the Iona Community. To this day in the
> islands, you'll find a certain reserve with incomers, of any description.
> White settlers, especially white settlers with dog collars, are still
> regarded with some aloofness.'
> – *Douglas Alexander*

But it wasn't the men with dog collars who felt that aloofness most keenly. It was their wives. Many of the women who accompanied their husbands – be they ministers or craftsmen – to Iona found it difficult to find acceptance among the islanders.

Master mason Bill Amos brought his young wife to live on Iona in the 1940s. Their son, Bill, remembers how difficult it was for her:

> 'When my mother first arrived on Iona, they stayed in a croft up at
> the North End, and the people she stayed with basically spoke noth-
> ing but Gaelic. They did have English, but they spoke nothing but

Gaelic, so that my mother didn't know what they were talking about. I know that, to some extent, if you were brought up speaking Gaelic, it was a big barrier to being accepted anywhere else. But it was used as a kind of reverse barrier. This was a way to keep people out. It was all they had, and it was used quite deliberately.'
– *Bill Amos*

When Joyce Alexander's husband, Douglas, was Warden of Community House, they spent a summer at the Abbey. She too encountered the closed nature of island society:

'There was almost an embarrassment about knowing who you were. It was a weird business: you could walk in and around the village, and some people just would make it obvious that you were not to be spoken to. Now, if you meet in the hills in the West Highlands, you say, "Hello, isn't it a lovely day?" or "Did you see the golden eagle?" But that wasn't true on Iona. And also there were certain people among the islanders that you didn't talk about to their neighbours, because they'd fallen out three generations back. It was all just a new world to me, and I kept putting my foot in it.'
– *Joyce Alexander*

Douglas Galbraith, a 'New Man' in the 1950s, also failed to find acceptance among the islanders:

'That was a great embarrassment to me, and it has remained so ever since. In fact, it's almost a painful thing, and sometimes makes me want to avoid Iona altogether. As a child, we had always gone to Highland communities on holiday, and I always felt very much a part of those communities. I remember being hugely affirmed, and touched, when somebody's collie dog put its paw on my knee, and the other people saying, "That means you're accepted." I even remember the collie dog's name – "Shira"! This was in the West Highlands, in Wester Ross. But on Iona, the divide had been set earlier than us, and even though the dances in the village hall worked well – we always went to them, and there was a certain kind of cordial arrangement with those who ran the dances – underneath that, there was a certain boundary that couldn't be crossed, almost a racial boundary that makes people

not know how to communicate with another group of people.'
– *Douglas Galbraith*

Although it was painful to many members of the Community, most understood only too well the reasons for the islanders' arm's length response:

'Here were all these people coming in and changing it all, and in a community like that, it's difficult to have changes.'
– *Ursula MacLeod*

'I think it's the old thing about incomers. It's a kind of, "What right have they got to be here? What right have they got to come in and change the way that we are? What was wrong with the Abbey just getting sorted out at the beginning of the century, and just having it like that for people who were interested? And what's wrong with a few artists, or other people, coming up here in the summer, and giving a wee boost to our income? There's nothing wrong with that, because they don't change anything. They don't interfere. They're not going to marry our children, and take them away. Nothing's going to be altered too much." That was my feeling: that it was a radical change that wasn't welcome, because it was a radical change. It wouldn't have mattered what it was.'
– *Bill Amos*

'The poor islanders, you know, would have to have been great Christians to have coped with some of the impositions. And George MacLeod, of course, although he was a Highlander through and through, and had been going to Iona for many years before he thought of establishing the Community, was someone who didn't let things stand still for very long. When there was a problem, it had to be solved, and he got on with solving it. And although he was very gracious and respectful to the islanders, it was inevitable that this imposition would cause tensions. This invasion, this alien invasion almost, of all kinds of people from mainland cities and from abroad, all centring on the Abbey, all making demands on the infrastructure of the island – a very small island – a tiny island, in fact – with a water

problem for one thing, and various other difficulties, particularly during the war. All told, I think the islanders coped remarkably well.'
– John Sim

Even the Community's rebuilding of the Abbey brought about changes which were unwelcome at first. Pat Macdonald got to know the island when her husband, Uist, joined the Community:

'It was a bit difficult for the islanders, in many ways, because, you see, Iona had been a place of pilgrimage for a long time, and people have a peculiar way of liking to see ruins. And this was going to be totally different.'
– Pat Macdonald

'The Community also purloined stones from the wall round about. Mind you, half of Iona had been built from stones from the Abbey, but that was by the way, and so there was a disturbance there.'
– George Wilkie

The decision by the Community to buy several properties on the island in order to establish a base for their work on Iona also caused some resentment among the islanders:

'The Community was probably completely unaware of the impact it would have on a small island, because you've got to remember that the Iona Community at that point in time was probably, with the exception of Uist Macdonald, a very Central Belt of Scotland organisation. And, in those days, you didn't own your houses in the Central Belt, or very few people did. But even in those days, the crofters on Iona had security of tenure, because the folk fought and went to jail to get them that.'
– Davie Kirkpatrick

Other simple, human misunderstandings would lead to resentment too. One of the first jobs John Jardine was ever asked to do on Iona was to prepare for the arrival of a group of young people who were going to be camping at the North End of the island, as part of the Community's youth programme:

'Up at the North End we had to set up the tents. A marquee for the girls, and a marquee for the boys. So we set up the tents, and then we had to clean out the wells, because the water came from outside wells. There was a well on the down side of the road, facing east, as it were. That was not too difficult, because the old lady who lived there, Betsy Ferguson, used that herself. But the one on the other side of the road was more difficult, because it was just used by cattle. We worked on that for a bit, and then Duncan MacArthur, who was the crofter on Achabhaich, thought we were interfering with the cattle's water supply. Duncan came and shouted at us for taking the water away from the cows. So that was an altercation over that, until Tom [Milroy] finally convinced him, and mollified him, and explained that it was nothing to do with upsetting the cows. That, in fact, once we had finished work, the water would be far cleaner for the cows, as well as for the campers. So that was all smoothed out.'
– *John Jardine*

As John suggests, this was a low-level misunderstanding with short-term consequences. Though, given that Iona was an island on which fresh water was a scarce commodity, the Community ought to have anticipated the anxiety that would be caused by their doing any unscheduled work on the wells. Like many other misunderstandings, its basis appears to have been in a failure to communicate properly with the islanders.

Fortunately, there was one islander who played a vital role in defusing potential misunderstandings between island community and Iona Community:

'Morag MacPhail, who was the postmistress, was one of these steadfast people. Very dependable. Very influential, I think, among her peers. And I liked her. There was something very solid and real about her.'
– *Joan Low*

'Morag was one of the people who, somehow, had a wonderful knack of relieving tensions. She was a communicator. She communicated to the Community problems which they may have not realised they were creating. She communicated to the islanders understandings of what

the Community were trying to do. And there were times, of course, when she really saved certain quite serious situations from developing.'
– *John Sim*

It's not clear why Morag was more willing than other islanders to give the Community a hearing, but Ursula MacLeod provides a clue:

'Morag MacPhail was a nurse, but she hadn't been able to finish doing her nursing training, because there had been a family crisis, and she had to come home.'
– *Ursula MacLeod*

The fact that Morag had lived on the mainland when she was training, and had had the opportunity to experience a different culture, may well have made her more open to change and to new ideas. Certainly, young wives and mothers like Joyce Alexander appreciated her acceptance of them:

'Morag was very friendly. Block House was a place that you could go. There were loads of ornaments and wee "footery"[18] things, so I didn't go that often, because I was always terrified that the kids would knock something precious off. But the Post Office and Block House was somewhere that you could go.'
– *Joyce Alexander*

Davie Kirkpatrick's mother, Nan, was also a friend of the Community:

'Nan never called me anything but Dr Joyce. But she wasn't an islander.'
– *Joyce Alexander*

Perhaps Nan herself had found it hard to find acceptance when she first came to the island. Other incomers did. Abbey cook Ursula MacLeod has never forgotten one particular boy:

'There was a young boy on one of the farms. He was an orphan, and he was one of these "boarded out" boys. He had very bad varicose veins, and he had to go away and have an operation. And the people he worked with were furious about this, and there was some unpleasantness about that boy. But he used to come into the kitchen every night, and sit. He was only about sixteen or seventeen, and he had no

home. No family. It was awful.'
– *Ursula MacLeod*

Sometimes, of course, relationships were pragmatic – at least, initially:

'There were one or two islanders who were very sympathetic: people like Doodie MacFadyen, who did things for us, carried stuff, and were very helpful. So relationships were being built up, more on a business basis than any other.'
– *Graeme Brown*

Davie Kirkpatrick's father, Charlie, who relied on his boat for a living, initially ventured out of the Island camp and into the Community camp, for pragmatic reasons too:

'My father was a man of independent thought, and I suppose he had to be realistic as well. We weren't in the lucky position to have croft land, or farmland, and, at that time, lobster was a luxury item, so you couldn't really sell lobsters into France, or even into the south of England. Even the boat trips at that point in time were difficult: there was only a very short season, middle of May to the middle of September, so he had to do something to feed his family, and he went to work for the Iona Community.'
– *Davie Kirkpatrick*

However, according to Davie, somewhere along the way his father's relationship with the Community changed from pragmatic to personal:

'My father was killed when I was very young – 1955. He was killed unloading the puffer, working for the Iona Community. But one of the things I remember very vaguely is my mother saying that she thought that, most probably, he would have joined the Iona Community, if he had lived.'
– *Davie Kirkpatrick*

The development of Charlie Kirkpatrick's relationship with the Community points to the fact that, despite all the impediments, individual members of the Community did build successful relationships with individual islanders.

A few, like Cameron Wallace, married into island families; but by far the most significant friendships were formed by Uist Macdonald. He understood and valued the islanders, and his wife, Pat, believes that it was his ability to relate to the islanders that was the glue that held the two camps together in the early years:

'Uist was able to be a great help there, because, of course, he spoke Gaelic, and, therefore, he was able to go round and speak to people. And, being the person he was, he went to every house. He had known some of them before, because he'd been there on holiday with his parents. And they would have known his father who was a well-known Gaelic minister. I think Uist helped to keep things fairly smooth.'
– *Pat Macdonald*

Uist's son-in-law, Leith Fisher, confirms the importance of Uist's contribution:

'He had a rapport between himself and the islanders that George MacLeod in his Olympian and, maybe, despotic way didn't quite. He was close friends with a lot of people on the island, and would visit them, share with them, talk to them in Gaelic, pray with them in Gaelic. He always saw that as important.'
– *Leith Fisher*

Uist's daughter, Nonie, also got to know the islanders well, through her father:

'I suppose, because there had always been links with our family and the island people, I knew some of them quite well. Mum and Dad always used to go and visit people around the island when we were on holiday.'
– *Nonie Fisher*

Ian Fraser believes that, without Uist, the Community would never have got off the ground:

'I think there could have been real trouble had Uist not been speaking their own language in their houses, making personal relation with

people. I think Uist provided a lifeline there that helped the Community to get on its way.'
– *Ian Fraser*

There were, of course, other early members of the Community who formed close ties of friendship with the locals. Douglas Alexander was one of them:

'The summer of 1959, the Iona Community sent a five-a-side football team, for the first time ever, to take part in the Tobermory Highland Games. And the five-a-side football team which went to Tobermory consisted of myself, Colin Morton, Ronnie Samuel [both ministers], young Hugh Lamont, who was one of the joiner craftsmen, and Gordon Grant. Gordon Grant is a well-kent figure on the island. He was a local crofter then. But Gordon Grant was not just the centre half of our football team, he was a friend. And there was young Ken Tindal, and, of course, Morag MacPhail. They were close friends, as well as being neighbours on the island.'
– *Douglas Alexander*

And Davie Kirkpatrick remembers times in the 1960s when the resident Community offered hospitality to the islanders:

'I think the first television that came to Iona was bought by Joan Isemonger who was cooking up at the Abbey at that point in time. Now Joan Isemonger was a very independent-thinking lady. She was a ferry pilot during the last war, bringing the bombers across to this country for us to use against the Germans, so she was a strong character. But anyway, the television came in, and the aerial went on the front of the Abbey. (Historic Scotland would have a hairy canary today if you stuck a television aerial in front of the Abbey!) But I remember Dr Grey from along at the end of the village going up, and all those kind of folk, and it was the boxing they went to see. There was a John Young there at that time, and it was his job, because he was not particularly interested in the boxing, to go down and shift the aerial. Because the picture came from Kirk O' Shotts, and the weather did play a big part in whether you got a good picture or not. And, of course, at the crucial minute, it would usually fail. So there was usually a big gathering of

Iona men at that point in time, and that drew people in that normally wouldn't have gone near the Iona Community.'
– *Davie Kirkpatrick*

What all these relationships have in common is that they were, and are, real friendships. Molly Harvey, who is one of those who has close friends among the islanders, believes that this has perhaps been the Community's best gift to the island:

'Undoubtedly, the Iona Community has brought to the island a lot of very good friendships, apart from anything else, and I think people on the island would be the first to say that. And I think that's the point: that if people get to know each other as individual people, face to face, and not as "Iona Community" and "Island", then a lot of hurt and resentment is broken down.'
– *Molly Harvey*

In retrospect, it is doubtful whether there is anything that George MacLeod and the early members of the Community could have done to minimise the tensions which developed. Tor Justad, who became involved in the Community's youth work right at the end of the 1960s, had the advantage of being able to build on the experience of those who had gone before him over the previous 30 years. But he had another advantage too:

'I was very lucky, because I actually lived in the village of Iona, in the main street, in a small "chalet", I suppose you'd call it, called Cul Cul Shuna. There's a house that is owned by the Community called Shuna, and behind that there was another house called Cul Shuna, and behind that there was another house called Cul Cul Shuna.

So I lived in the chalet there, which obviously gave me an advantage, in the sense that you were seen in the village all the time, and you got to know your neighbours, and you met people as you walked along the street. And I suppose I was always a little bit critical of what I saw, at times, as the isolation of the Abbey from the islanders, and from island life in general. I don't think it was necessarily people being deliberately isolationist, but probably more a case of not making the

proactive efforts that I think you would need to make, in order to be more closely linked to the islanders.'
– *Tor Justad*

However, Tor does not underestimate how difficult it would have been, in practical terms, to establish those links:

'Having said that, in the summer season, both the people working in the Community and the islanders were tremendously busy, whether it was looking after their croft, or their B&B, or their shop, or whatever, so that the opportunities for dialogue, apart from greeting people on the street, were fairly limited.

Interestingly, in the winter, the opportunities were probably greater, because people had more time, but then again there weren't so many people from the Community living on the island then. So it was a sort of chicken and egg one, in the sense that, in the winter the opportunity was there, but there weren't as many people there, and those that were there had their specific jobs to do, and didn't necessarily see contact with the [local] community as part of their remit. Their time was spent getting to know the people that they were working with on a daily basis. So the idea of having, on top of that, to go out and make contact with people they had never seen before was difficult.'
– *Tor Justad*

John Sim, who first lived and worked at the Abbey in the 1940s, confirms Tor's analysis:

'Well, I didn't see much of the islanders really, because my whole life was centred round the Abbey. This was 1946, and I was there for three months. I did get to know a few of the islanders, but mainly I was with the Community people.'
– *John Sim*

And Ian Mackenzie observed the same phenomenon a decade later:

'There was constant restiveness between the villagers – the islanders –

and the Community. I often felt the Community was guilty of ...
what? ... indifference? They had their own big, big thing. It was very
hard work for everybody, and they just had to keep going.'
– *Ian Mackenzie*

In truth, the Community's vision was so vast, and the working out of that
vision so all-encompassing, that it was bound to lead to difficult relationships with the local people. Douglas Galbraith certainly can't imagine
how they could have avoided conflict:

'I remember thinking at the time how difficult that would be, because
of the nature of the vision, and recognising that people like George
MacLeod who have visions of this kind, inevitably displace other
things when they're achieving them. Therefore, there might not have
been any way of moving gently into partnership with the local
community, when you wanted to do these radical things with their
island.

Of course there were members of the Community who achieved that:
the Industrial Chaplain Cameron Wallace, for example. And I think
people wanted to, but unless you were lucky, you didn't find a way of
doing that. But people like Cameron did leave a kind of deposit of
possibility. I'm sure we tried to build on it, but there was always the
wariness.'
– *Douglas Galbraith*

The challenge for the Community is to continue to build on that 'deposit
of possibility'. It won't be easy. There is still a wariness among the
islanders, and a feeling that the contribution of the islanders to the
enduring appeal of Iona has been overlooked:

'A lot of the people that come through the Iona Community don't
think that they need the people of Iona. But part of that fabric of Iona
that people admire, or feel, is due to the present and past population
of Iona.'
– *Davie Kirkpatrick*

Davie clearly feels that the part played by the local population in the stewardship of Iona has never been properly acknowledged. And at least one of the early members agrees.

Ian Fraser, who first came to Iona in 1939, observes that, while George MacLeod did make serious attempts to explain his vision to the islanders, 'the fact that they'd been there before him didn't seem to occur to him'.

Perhaps it's not too late for the Iona Community to acknowledge the contribution of the local community – and help revive their vision of the island.

3

Photos

1. The village, Iona, 1939 (Raymond Bailey archive)

2. The jetty, Iona, 1940 (Duncan Finlayson archive)

3. George MacLeod outside the Abbey, 1939 (Raymond Bailey archive)

4. Morag MacPhail outside the Iona Post Office (Molly Harvey archive)

5. The Parish Kirk, 1958 (Molly Harvey archive)

6. Dunsmeorach, 1958 (Molly Harvey archive)

7. Charlie Kirkpatrick and family (Joe Hislop archive)

8. The dedication of the rebuilt Abbey precincts (Molly Harvey archive)

9. Uist (centre) and Pat Macdonald (Pat Macdonald archive)

The Community
and women

If one thing is clear from interviews with early members of the Iona Community, it is that virtually none of them questioned its all-male policy. It was, after all, a community of ministers and craftsmen, all of whom were male in the 1940s and '50s:

> 'In these days, I doubt if there was any move at all for women even to become deacons in the Church. There were some women who were working as deaconesses, as they called them. They were lay workers doing various jobs, missionary work in the Church. And there were women missionaries out in foreign fields, but the idea of a woman becoming an elder or a minister still hadn't moved over the horizon. Any more than a married woman going out to work had really been considered. So when we were in the Iona Community as males, we thought it was perfectly natural that it should be a male preserve.'
> – *John Sim*

> 'It was a male-dominated "everything". I liked women, but it would never have occurred to me. That's the astonishing thing – the way that you can take utterly for granted an injustice. But that was the paradigm: all institutions were male dominated. There were women around when I did join the Community. There were lots of lovely, interesting women there who happened to be the wives of the ministers, but I never paused to think about it.'
> – *Richard Holloway*

Even more striking is the almost complete acceptance by those women themselves of the fact that there would be no place for them in this new Community:

> 'The role of women was really non-existent in the Community at that time, and, looking back, I must have been very naïve and very unthinking, because it didn't really make a big impact on me. And I don't think it was an issue among many of the wives of people who were joining. I think a lot of us felt, at that time, that we were part of it, just because our husbands were members. And that's pathetic looking back now!'
> – *Molly Harvey*

'In a way, we were unquestioning. I mean, I didn't get too bugged about it. I can't say that it brought out a whole lot of raised feminist hackles, because I don't suppose I knew I had any feminist hackles at that point.'
– *Chris McGregor*

'Looking back on that now, I think, "Why the hell did you not get in there and ginger them up?" My kids think it's mad. And looking back, it was mad. But because George MacLeod was the driving force behind it, and in many ways it was his decision, not the Community's decision, none of us ever baulked at it.'
– *Joyce Alexander*

'He was starting it off with this group of a dozen men: craftsmen and ministers. Women weren't ministers, and women weren't carpenters. I don't think it would ever have occurred to him, and if it had occurred to him, he'd have certainly said, "No way!"'
– *Molly Harvey*

George's son Maxwell believes that his father's attitude can be attributed to the experiences of his childhood and young adulthood:

'He went to Cargilfield [Prep School] which was all-male, then he went to Winchester [Public School] which was all-male, then he went to Oxford which was all-male, and then he went to recruit camp with the Argyll and Sutherland Highlanders which was all-male. So you have a situation of a man who had virtually no inter-relationship with women.'
– *Maxwell MacLeod*

George's ease with men and unease with women was obvious to everyone who came into contact with him:

'George was a man's man, and he was terrific with men, and encouraged them, and there was no doubt that he was charismatic as far as men were concerned. But he was remarkably awkward with women. He really didn't manage women very well. If you were walking back and forward to the Abbey, and you saw George ahead of you, if you

were a young man, you would seize your moment, and fall into step, and get the richness from him. But – well, I'll speak for myself – I would slow my pace, and think, "Oh no, I'm not going to put myself through that," because he was very awkward with ladies. And not only was he awkward himself directly with women, he really didn't understand how other men felt about women, so it was really quite difficult.'
– *Chris McGregor*

But while the wives of early members seem to have been tolerant of George's difficulty with women, and accepted that they could not be members of the Community, the issues were, perhaps, more sharply focussed for women who were not wives. Women like Alice Scrimgeour, a deaconess working in a deprived area in Glasgow, who had actually been on Iona in 1938, and had heard about this proposed Community at first-hand:

'I was particularly interested in George saying that Govan wasn't really being a parish church, because it was ignoring the poor people in the parish. And I got excited then, and I wrote him a wee letter saying I was a Church Sister in an East End church, and I was very interested. So he said, "We must have a meeting of Church Sisters some day." But it took us until 1947 to have a meeting of Church Sisters!'
– *Alice Scrimgeour*

As it turned out, Alice, herself, didn't have to wait nine years to have a meeting with George MacLeod. He invited her to Iona in 1943, to a Clubs' Conference to hear about the proposed Iona Youth Trust. A Mrs Morris from the Youth Committee went with her:

'She and I went up and experienced the "No Women" thing. They took what was the old Free Church manse. George hired it for these women that had to be looked after. We had our lunch and our dinner at the Columba Hotel, but we made our own breakfast on an old kitchen range.'
– *Alice Scrimgeour*

But while the women were not allowed to eat with the men up at the Abbey, they were still expected to help prepare their food:

'Miss Buchan and I were put on to the kitchen job: the cutting up of the vegetables for soup. We weren't excluded from the work of the Community! It was this kind of "second-class citizen" thing that made me annoyed. I wasn't a second-class citizen at home. There was no nonsense about Dad. He really admired Mother very much, and there was no difference in their relationship with each other. So I was astounded at this second-class citizenship.'
– *Alice Scrimgeour*

This strict segregation of men and women was enforced even in the most extreme circumstances. Ian Renton joined the Community at a particularly difficult time for him personally:

'My wife was in a pregnant state, living in a house in the village, and we weren't allowed to meet each other much, so it wasn't entirely a happy year. That was in August, and the baby was born in September.'
– *Ian Renton*

Other women chafed at this enforced segregation too. Stewart McGregor's fiancée, Chris, vividly remembers how it felt to be excluded. She made a special journey to see Stewart during his first summer on Iona:

'The first time we went, I was arriving on my birthday, and Stewart met me at the jetty, and he said, "I've got bad news." And I said, "What's that?" "Oh, George has said we are to be in silent retreat all weekend." So, of course, I was blowing my top all weekend, because we were going to have a birthday party, and that was it. George had said that the "New Men" [ministers] all had to be in silent retreat, and not speak from Friday evening, so Stewart was even breaking the rules by telling me on the Saturday.'
– *Chris McGregor*

Chris never did get her birthday party, but while women like Chris and Alice Scrimgeour fumed inwardly, neither felt that she could do anything about it:

'I thought it was terrible. And I couldn't see any way out of it. You see, George thought of it as ministers' training, and we were not allowed

to be ministers either. We talked among ourselves about it, but I never said to George. I think he knew within himself that we laughed a bit about it, in a derogatory kind of way. And the club leaders, Jessie Adamson and others, would talk to him about it – and some of the young men.'
– *Alice Scrimgeour*

The urging of the young men at last prevailed, because, however reluctantly, George eventually agreed to the formation of the Women Associates. This was, however, a sop. Adam Campbell, one of the craftsmen who worked on the Abbey at that time, summed it up neatly:

'Well, the Women Associates, they gave falls for the pulpits and that. They never got staying at the Abbey.'
– *Adam Campbell*

Actually, Adam is not strictly accurate. The Women Associates were allowed to stay in the Abbey on two specific occasions each year: for one week in May, in order to get everything shipshape for the arrival of the men, and for one week in September, to clean up after they had gone.

This is not to denigrate the work of the Women Associates – they were as enthused by George MacLeod's vision as the young ministers were, and they contributed in the only way that was open to them. But Alice Scrimgeour was not impressed by the terms on which the Women Associates were allowed to participate:

'The people in the Associates, which I eventually joined, were always saying, "It's such a privilege! Such a privilege to be here!" And you had to grovel a bit – which is not my nature!'
– *Alice Scrimgeour*

So why did strong, motivated women like Alice Scrimgeour not press more strongly for full membership in the years that followed? One of the explanations offered by a number of them is that there were, at that time, two very prominent women who appeared to be both happy with their unofficial status, and still able to make a contribution to Community life:

'The obvious one is Jenny Morton. Jenny was at the centre of things,

but she was such an able thinker, and actor, and debater, that she was bound to be at the centre of things.'
– *George Wilkie*

Jenny Morton was the wife of Ralph Morton, Deputy Leader of the Community, and Joint Warden of Community House, the Iona Community's base in Glasgow, but not, of course, a member. Her daughter, Faith, observed at close quarters her mother's commitment to the Community:

'Officially, she was always very much on the sidelines, and when they went up to Iona, my father would be staying in the huts very often, with George MacLeod and the group of young ministers. Women were just allowed in occasionally. You were allowed to come and listen if there was some kind of open meeting going on, and so she was very much on the outside officially.

But, in practice, informally, she was a great hostess. Even when we were living in tents, she would have people from the Community coming up for a meal, and great discussions would take place there. And so she was very much in on the thinking, and knowing what was happening, even if there was no question of being a member of the Community at that stage.'
– *Faith Aitken*

Maxwell MacLeod remembers Jenny well:

'Jenny, I used to go and visit sometimes in her extraordinary tent at the North End, which was designed for fifty soldiers or something. And she'd be in there with her huge bed, and her desk, and, beneath her, the great white sands of the North End of the island. It was wonderful for a child. This was the way to camp, obviously. And I remember having dinner there too. She was quite famous for her hospitality.'
– *Maxwell MacLeod*

Salubrious tent notwithstanding, it was no easy matter to cater for dozens of people at the North End of the island:

'They just had this small Calor gas stove in the tent. It was quite complicated in those days, because food supplies weren't all that easy

there, so that a lot of it came by post. She would send up food parcels from Glasgow. Bread was ordered from the bakers in Oban, and parcels of bread came in the post, or on the "King George" [steamer]. And, of course, you'd no fridges or anything in a tent, so I think we used tins a lot. It was quite difficult to get fresh vegetables on the island. Mary Ann at the shop did grow some lettuces in Iona Cottage, and sometimes, if you were lucky, you were allowed to buy a lettuce from her, but I think most of the food was tins.'
– *Faith Aitken*

Carol Morton, who was later to become Jenny's daughter-in-law, was on the receiving end of her hospitality, while still a student. Right from the start, she could see the significance of Jenny's contribution:

'It was clear – terribly clear – staying with Jenny and Ralph, that Jenny participated in a very vital way, though not a member of the Community. As did other wives. But because she was resident there the whole summer, I think it made a tremendous difference, particularly in the lives of the "New Men", because she provided the social structure – having a certain number each night to dinner. And always starting off with a sherry! And just talking generally, and getting to know them as people, not just as members of the Iona Community. I think that was an invaluable service which rarely, if ever, has been recognised.'
– *Carol Morton*

The other prominent woman who appeared to be happy with her lot was George MacLeod's wife, Lorna. She and their children would accompany George to Iona every summer, and virtually everyone who met her describes her as being full of life and laughter.

Each year, a student would come up to help Lorna with the children while they were living at their Iona base, Dunsmeorach, and one of those students was Molly Harvey:

'There were a lot of laughs in Dunsmeorach; a lot of laughs and a lot of fun. Lorna would come lolloping down the stairs with a fag hanging out of the end of her mouth, and she'd say, "Hiya, Moll! What are we going to feed them all on today then?" She was a wonderful cook,

and she produced amazing meals just like that. And I really was so lucky to have those four summers.'
– *Molly Harvey*

Lorna's sister, Ursula, also remembers a house full of laughter:

'Lots of people stayed there. There was always one secretary. There was the lecturer, and his wife, if he had one. Perhaps another odd bod. It was very, very busy, and full of laughter and fun. There was a hatch between the kitchen and the dining room, and once, when the meal was over, and the professors were sitting having very intense conversations, my sister realised she'd left her cigarettes on the dining room table. So she decided she would go through the hatch and collect them off the table as quietly as possible. But, of course, it wasn't quiet!'
– *Ursula MacLeod*

Lorna's children agree that she was a vivacious, life-affirming person, but their assessment of the summers she spent in Dunsmeorach is more jaundiced:

'Her whole summer was having people staying in Dunsmeorach. It was really like a B&B. And it was a B&B without a washing machine. Imagine having to get the sheets ready for the next people, and enough food. And there were always disasters happening in Iona: people going mad, or alcoholics drinking too much, or dramas which had to be coped with. So my mother had to have this B&B, but also have it as a kind of steady rock for my father to come home to, usually at two in the morning. So I think my mother had a hard time.'
– *Mary MacLeod*

'My mother's greatest pleasure, being the daughter of a Highland parish minister, was keeping in with the gossip, and sitting on the pier, talking complete nonsense with her cronies as they came off the ferry. She just loved that. And I remember her saying to me one year, "I have been unable to get down to the ferry this year." A distance of a quarter of a mile! Because every single moment was washing dishes. It was like being on a huge safari: lots and lots of people around; primus lamps; no money. Some farmer used to come round and say

husbands. Some of them actually living rough with their children. Burnside Cottage, where the pottery is now, used to be four walls and a roof with rats, and some Community wives lived there, because there was nowhere else. Some people camped. Some people slept in barns, because they could not afford to live on a croft. And they did that so as not to be separated from their husbands. Some people have very bad memories of that time.'
– Isabel Whyte

Ena Kellet has bad memories:

'Our husbands were joining the Community, but we were really a nuisance, being on the island. I think George MacLeod would have preferred it if the women hadn't been there. The year Jackie joined the Community, we went up, and we lived in the barn – Black's Barn. It was actually attached to the cowshed, and the dung was up the wall, and Jackie used to come down and help, because Lorna was wee and in nappies. And he used to help to wash the nappies under the cold tap. There wasn't a toilet: there was an "Elsie" [chemical toilet] outside, which was also disgusting, and an old black cooker.

I shared it with Jean McAlpine – I had two children, and she had one wee boy. We had to take all our own linen, and I laid the sheets on the bed, and they were covered with ticks! We had a very posh friend who said, "Oh my God, you're living like a refugee!" That's exactly what she said.'
– Ena Kellet

But it would be misleading to suggest that this is the whole story. Like Lorna MacLeod and Jenny Morton, these women redeemed their situation. They supported one another where they could, and, in the hardship and the loneliness, they somehow managed to find fun and laughter. They were a resilient lot:

'There was a lot that we had to learn to cope with: the "Elsies" which we hadn't been used to; the black stove which we had to collect wood for; and no decent cutlery, or cups and saucers, or anything like that. But we survived, and it's good to look back and think we were strong enough, and we were able to do it. And we did have good fun as well. We had folk for afternoon tea and coffee. And the children survived. We took them to the beach, and they played, and they loved it.

I borrowed a pram on Iona – you know the old Victorian pram? It didn't have any bottom on it, it was just rounded. Somebody gave me a loan of it, and I always remember I was pushing it up the hill towards Black's Barn, and Cecilia Levison came and helped me. I pushed that pram all round the island. It was a difficult time, but I wasn't unhappy, because I had a friend, Jean McAlpine, and we laughed about a lot of things. We did laugh.'
– *Ena Kellet*

'I went up one year, and we took the house called Lovedale in the main street. It belonged to one of the islanders, a lady who lived on her own at the time, and the story was that she spent the winter in the house with the hens for company. We made the mistake of taking Lovedale in the month of June, because, of course, it emerged that the tenants who came in June cleaned the house for the rest of the people. At this point, I had a nearly two-year-old, and was quite heavily pregnant, and this house was really in quite a state. So I had to set-to and clean, and, of course, I had to go along to the village shop, which was Mary Ann's in these days, and buy things like – well, they weren't called "Ajax", they were called "Whizz" and "Boom" and stuff like that! And I went along one day and I pointed to the "Whizz" or the "Boom", and said, "Another bottle of that." And she said, "I'm not selling you any more. You've cleaned enough." She just refused point-blank to sell me any more!'
– *Chris McGregor*

The struggles on Iona were good preparation for the life of an Extension Parish minister's wife. It too presented unique challenges. When Ena and Jack Kellet moved into the manse at Menzieshill in Dundee, the houses were still being built:

'There weren't roads: there was just mud, and snow, and a few houses. We had an open door – we really did. We should have had revolving doors! The house was open and people knew it, and I think that was

why we still have friends we keep in touch with from our first parish. Mind you, it wasn't all easy. We didn't have any money. The other day, a friend of mine said, "Remember when Jimmy Shand came when we were opening the halls, and raising money for the church? You took the curtains down from your back bedroom and made a dress!" That's what I did. So they were hard times as well, and very busy times. Jackie was out a lot. Every night. It isn't all easy when you're building up a new church. Jackie worked very hard. The priest moved into the parish, and the ladies said to him, "You'll have to visit Ena and Jack. They visit us." And so the parish priest came for his supper nearly every night, when Jackie was out working. And he used to sit beside the fire, or he would help to bath the bairns. He said, "It's very comfortable here." He was a lonely man. But he didn't go out every night visiting. Jackie went out every night, knocking on doors.'
– *Ena Kellet*

George Charlton also worked hard to put into practice the kind of systematic parish visitation that George MacLeod had taught him to do:

'He'd come in when the wee ones were away to bed, and then I'd be sitting up 'til yon time. There were certain homes that he would go to that he wouldn't come in until eleven, twelve o'clock, and I'm knitting, and waiting for him coming home, and discover that I'd fallen asleep and all the stitches were off my needle.'
– *Dorothy Charlton*

But again, despite the difficulties, these women achieved great things in the parishes, in their own right:

'In Menzieshill, we started the first pre-school playgroup. There wasn't another one in Dundee. Ours was the first. And we raised a lot of money, and we bought first-class equipment. We fought for juice and milk with the Council, and they eventually gave it to us. And from that time, pre-school playgroups developed.'
– *Ena Kellet*

It's difficult now to trace the exact moment when these women first challenged the all-male membership of the Community, but it is clear that the

Community's Economic Rule was a catalyst. Some wives accepted it –
others resented it bitterly:

'It never occurred to me to join, or to want to join: it wasn't an issue.
And yet, looking back, we then were part of an economic discipline,
and I suppose if you hadn't been in tune and in sympathy with that, it
could have been very difficult for wives.'
– *Molly Harvey*

It was certainly a sticking point for many, including Isabel Whyte, who
desperately wanted to participate in the full life of the Community with
her husband, Iain:

'"Ah well," I said, "if I can't be a member of the Community, my earn-
ings shouldn't be taken into account," and that was what we agreed.'
– *Isabel Whyte*

John Sim explains what happened next:

'To attempt an economic discipline had its problems, particularly
when you had wives struggling to make ends meet in bringing up a
family – feeding them, and dressing them, and so on. Now I think a
number of the women, the wives, really felt, "This is all very well,
these men laying down the law, making the rules, but we're the ones
who've got to cope with the actual challenge of this. We want a say in
this matter as well." And after a comparatively short time, it became
obvious that there was a demand for Family Groups to meet and
discuss Community issues. So they set up Family Groups in various
parts of the country, where ministers and their wives met together
and discussed all kinds of issues, including the economic discipline.
That was the beginning. That was the impetus for change.'
– *John Sim*

Gradually then, the tide began to turn, until by the 1960s, many
members realised that the all-male policy was a problem that had to be
addressed:

'To those of us who joined in 1959 it was not a problem. There was no

hassle. Within five years, it had become an issue of real tension and contention. And looking back, if I may bear my soul, I did not appreciate, personally, how important it was for the Community to move forward from its all-male stance. I came late to the fold, and I've no hesitation, although I have some embarrassment, in admitting that. But in that, I was also, I think, accompanied by George MacLeod.'
– Douglas Alexander

In the end, however, even George MacLeod had to give way to an unstoppable force:

'Iona meant a lot to me, and I had accepted the rules, and not really challenged too many of them at that stage. But then they started to discuss whether women should be admitted to the Community, and we had a furious argument. In 1968! In nearly everything else the Community has been way ahead of the Church of Scotland: in its peace witness, in its social concerns, in its involvement in urban areas, and so on. And here they were against something which certainly I've always seen as a matter of human rights, and I suppose I was just beginning to see it as that in the Community.'
– Isabel Whyte

'By that time I had been a Church of Scotland minister's wife for a little while, and it was clear all the organisations were split according to gender – which didn't seem to me the best way to go about things. But we were in a small working-class community, and it wasn't my role to change that kind of thing. But I did think that the Community, if it was to be a new way of speaking to people – not just men – could be a bit more progressive in that way. Major decisions were being made which, after all, were affecting my life as much as Colin's! And I wasn't alone, obviously, in speaking that way.'
– Carol Morton

'I remember it was Mollie Hood, whose husband, Stanley, had joined, who first said, "You know, I want to join. I'm going to join this!" And that certainly got me thinking, and I thought, "Well, good on her! Maybe we do need to join, and then I would really be a member of this Community in my own right, never mind just tagging along as

part of John.'''
– *Molly Harvey*

The first woman became a member in 1969, and it appears that George MacLeod gave in less than gracefully:

'I was working as a volunteer in the Abbey, just about the time that the first women joined the Community, and, by this time, I was a very radically feminist 18-year-old. George used to invite volunteers who were working in the Abbey – well, he used to invite the male volunteers – to come to his room for sherry, and he would talk to them about joining the Iona Community when they had finished university, or whatever. But he never invited the girls, so I gatecrashed this meeting one day. I went along with some of the male volunteers into his room. He opened the door, and I just went in. However, I was out, before my feet could touch the ground really.'
– *Kathy Galloway*

Interestingly, George MacLeod seems to have taken a different attitude to the women who were employed by the Community. In her battle to be accepted as an equal to the men who were involved in the Community's youth work, Alice Scrimgeour found an unexpected ally:

'The first time the Community ran a training course, George MacNeill was the Secretary for the Iona Youth Trust, and he decided he would run it. And he ran it, and A.M. Scrimgeour got little chance. I sat in the audience most of the time, and yet I was the Clubs' Organiser for the Church for the West of Scotland!

So when the next course was being talked about, I said I would need to have a bigger part in it. George MacNeill was mad, but he had to give in, because George MacLeod backed me up. And he did a lot of little things after that.'
– *Alice Scrimgeour*

Many people offered various theories as to why George MacLeod remained so implacably opposed to women members, but by far the most convincing were the stories told by those who had observed, at first-hand, his effect on some women:

Annie Price was thirteen years old when George MacLeod moved from his church in Edinburgh to Govan Old in 1930:

'The church was packed and, of course, he had a great following of ladies who fancied him, and came from Edinburgh.'
– *Annie Price*

Raymond Bailey, who accompanied George to Iona in 1939, observed the same phenomenon, when George MacLeod based himself on the island for the summer:

'He was tall and handsome, and women just swooned round him. And, in Iona, it was a deliberate effort to keep them at arm's length. That was why he didn't have them in the Community. To have women in the Community would have destroyed it for him at that point, and whether he was conscious of it or not, he probably realised that he would be personally in a very difficult situation. That he'd have these young women swooning round him as members. Even older women. In a sense, it was a defence of his own purity.'
– *Raymond Bailey*

In effect, famous preachers were treated like rock stars in those days, and George MacLeod had to contend with his fair share of groupies and stalkers, as his daughter, Mary, remembers:

'Women were always falling in love with my father. He always had women panting after him in some form or other. My mother put up with a lot of women who were in love with him. I know that was difficult for her, because we would have people – I mean, really, we would have a lot of people – wanting him all the time – wanting his time and attention. And certain people feeling very strongly about him. I don't quite know what conversations went on between them, but it must have been difficult.

I think a lot of it was couched in terms of "churchiness". These were not wives of Iona Community members, I'd like to emphasise! They were rather strange women – who would ring him constantly – I mean, constantly – and always want to be speaking to him. I think there was a pretext of seeing him, on her own, about some kind of intellectual or spiritual matter. He was very cool, but I think that was very attractive to women, so it was counterproductive really. I think he dealt with it – he interpreted it – as a spiritual need.

There were people who, I think, really truly believed that they were married to my father, and I know of two women who called them-selves "Lady MacLeod" at that time, and they would have cheque books in that name.

And once, when I was quite young, I remember coming home with my mother, and this woman was in the house with a knife, waiting to kill my mother, because she was in the way. I remember being shut in the sitting room with my mother, realising my father was out there with this woman who was – I want to get dramatic and say she actu-ally put a knife into the door, but I'm not quite sure that actually happened – but I remember it being very dramatic.

There was a German woman too that used to come up to Iona, and she always found out when he was going to be on the island. He used to put up a timetable of when people could speak to him, so she, of course, would be there and have her name on the timetable, so he was ensconced with her for some time. The joke is that my mother put her name up to see him for two hours during the day, and he was furi-ous with her. But, you know, she went up, and he would be sitting in the Abbey talking to women who would be pouring out their soul. Very difficult – for both actually.'
– *Mary MacLeod*

Seen in this light, MacLeod's arm's length approach to women, however damaging its effect on others, appears to have been, essentially, a coping mechanism.

Despite these mitigating factors, however, what remains puzzling is just how a visionary like George MacLeod, and a Community so wholeheart-edly committed to social justice, could be so blind, for so long, to the merits of the case for women's full participation in the Community.

1

2

5

6

9

10

Photos

1. The craftsmen gather at the jetty at 5:30am to watch Joe Blair pipe George MacLeod off the island, on his way to his wedding in 1949 (Joe Blair archive)

2. George MacLeod's Secretary, Miss McKinnon (left), with Alice Scrimgeour (centre), Iona, 1949 (Patsy Colvin archive)

3. The Women Associates (Faith Aitken archive)

4. Jenny Morton (left) with Ralph Morton, aboard the yacht 'Tectona' (Faith Aitken archive)

5. Ursula MacLeod with 'Sooty' on the steps of Dunsmeorach (Molly Harvey archive)

6. Lorna MacLeod with Mary in the pram, and Mary Tolland (standing) (Duncan Finlayson archive)

7. John and Beryl Jardine with son, Mark, in the pram, Iona, 1958 (Molly Harvey archive)

8. Lorna, Maxwell and Mary MacLeod with George's Secretary, Miss MacKenzie, and Ross Mathers (Molly Harvey archive)

9. Maxwell MacLeod outside Dunsmeorach (Molly Harvey archive)

10. George MacLeod is engaged by women visitors to Iona (Faith Aitken archive)

The Community and the craftsmen

This is the story of the Community's rebuilding of the Abbey as told by five of the craftsmen, with a little help from two of the women who cooked their meals, and cared for them as if they were their own.

On being recruited

'In the autumn of 1938, Munich time,[19] I was working at the post office in Edinburgh, putting in beams and brick work, and Willie Amos [master mason] met me at the corner, and he says to me, "How would you like to go to Iona to work?" Well, I kind of hummed and hawed, and then my mother said, "If it does you nae good, it'll dae you nae harm."

So, Willie went to the trade union, and some masons were interested. You would read in some of the books that we were "a group of unemployed volunteers", and, to a certain extent, we were volunteers, but most of us left jobs to go.

Then Dr MacLeod arranged a meeting down at Acheson House [the Iona Community's Edinburgh HQ] and the Trade Union Secretary was there – a Mr Black. And Dr MacLeod told him that there were huts along the front of the Abbey, and each man would have a room and food, instead of "country money" – subsistence. Mr Black saw the plans we were going to build, and said, "Very good bit of building ahead of you." So after the meeting, it was all arranged.

Them that was going up, went to Govan Old in Glasgow, and had a wee service, and then we got the night train to Oban where we were allowed to stay until the "King George" [steamer] came. So we sailed round in the "King George", and saw our first view of the Abbey – four-square to the wind! I followed Uist Macdonald up the gangway with a bag of tools. That would be early June 1939.'
– *Adam Campbell*

'They couldn't get tradesmen during the war, so George MacLeod came up with the idea that Jimmy Bowman, who was our joinery teacher at Kilmarnock in the pre-apprenticeship course, would go up, and take four apprentices. So, in the class we had a vote, and I was fortunate to be one of the four who were selected to go to Iona. And it was a good feeling, right from the word go.

The journey up was really very interesting. We had to get a train from Buchanan Street in Glasgow, at nine o'clock at night, and travel overnight to Oban to get there in time for the ferry in the morning. And, of course, on the way up, because we were travelling overnight, it was difficult to get sleeping. Everybody said, "You'll be able to sleep on the train," and, of course, we couldn't sleep on the train. And the next idea was, "Well, it gets in very early to Oban in the morning, you'll be able to sleep then." But, of course, the cleaners came round. And so we were really suffering badly from sleep deprivation. Anyway, the next idea was, "Well, when we get onto the bus to go down the Ross [of Mull], we'll be able to sleep on that." But it was a utility bus[20] with these wooden-slat seats, so no way could you sleep in it!

Going through Glen More, it was torrential rain. It reminded me of the song about Mull, "Green grassy island of sparkling fountains",[21] because all the little burns running down the mountain were like silver streamers.

By the time we got to Bunessan, it started to clear up, and, after the rain, the atmosphere was so much clearer. So it was like going from black-and-white into a technicolour world. And by the time we got to Fionnphort, it was just absolutely brilliant. I can remember it as clear as anything. I remember sitting in the little ferry boat – it was just like an enlarged rowing boat really. I can remember sitting in the stern, and looking down through ten feet of water, and seeing the crabs crawling about in the sand, it was so clear.'
– *John Young*

'I served my apprenticeship in Prestwick, as a joiner with a small, local firm, and my idea was, eventually, to train to be a teacher of Technical Education. It so happened that there was a man lived in the same street where I was working as an apprentice, and in my final year, he came to the workshop, and he said, "How would you like to learn about barrel roofing?" So I said, "Where is this?" He said, "It's on Iona." Well, of course, I didn't know where Iona was. So anyway, he arranged for me to meet George MacLeod, and that would be about March 1948.

I went to Iona Community House in Clyde Street in Glasgow, and, lo and behold, when I got there, there was a meeting in progress. I met George MacLeod down on the ground floor, and he says, "Come up, I want you to meet Sir Stafford Cripps."[22] Well, I was flabbergasted, of course. Here was a joiner from Prestwick meeting Sir Stafford Cripps! I was introduced to him, and, from then on, things started to take shape. I came back home and told my parents what had happened, and that there was every possibility that I could be going to Iona to work on a barrel roof. And, of course, my parents didn't understand what I was blethering about. But, by the first of July, I was on my way to Iona, on board the "King George V".'
– *Joe Blair*

'I left school in 1953, and it was the following year that I went off to Iona. The first job I had was with a chap, building fences on Mull, and I was quite taken with it, and I quite enjoyed doing it. And then I came home this night, and my parents told me about this job on Iona, and I wasn't at all keen. Although we lived in Bunessan [on the Ross of Mull], I think I'd probably only been on Iona once, or maybe twice. Iona, to us kids anyway, was almost another planet. And, of course, all my school pals were in Bunessan, and going to Iona was going away from all that. Anyway, my parents were not the sort of parents who would insist on anything, but their advice prevailed, and I agreed that I would go to Iona.

When I went there, originally around about Easter time, it was just meant as a summer job, labouring to the masons. There was no mention of an apprenticeship, or a permanent job, at that point. But I must admit I very quickly adapted to life on Iona. I really enjoyed it, and I liked being at the Community. Of course, there were people there that I knew: there was big John Campbell, and Calum Macpherson, and Attie MacKechnie. I really took to it straight away, and, in fact, my parents remarked on how seldom I came back to Bunessan at weekends.

I worked very happily throughout the summer, and then, when it came August – my birthday's the 4th of August – I was offered the opportunity of the apprenticeship. That was something that I seized with both hands. I hadn't got any thoughts of anything like that, and it came out the blue, but I remember that I didn't have any problems making up my mind. I just agreed there and then, and that was it, signed, sealed and delivered. So then, after my birthday, we got a tool kit together, and I was working with the joiners. There was John Kane and John Thompson, the two joiners; there was also two other joiners who were just working there in the summertime, Davidson Sinclair and Tom Paterson. They were teachers, and they would go back to their teaching jobs when the schools opened in the autumn time. And the job that was being done at that moment was finishing off the inside of the East Range. That started my apprenticeship, and then it moved on from there to the restoration of the Relig Odhráin[23] and St Columba's Shrine.'

– *Hugh Lamont*

'Actually, how I got the job was: I was on construction work, and the job finished, and the next job I was getting wasn't starting until September, so I actually went to work on a farm, as a shepherd. But it was three weeks, and I hadn't been paid. So I asked one Saturday morning about my wages, and I was told, "Well, we'll have to wait for the bank, but we can give you £3 just now." So they gave me the £3, and I just jumped in my van, and away I went.

So I went into the hotel and had a pint, and the barman said, "Oh, you're finished early today." I said, "I've left. I've only got £3 for three weeks' work." And away home I went. And then who came to my door, but Calum Macpherson. He was the boss of all the workmen [at the Abbey], and he said to me, "Bob, would you like to come to Iona and work on the West Range?" I asked him what the deal was, and how the lodgings went, and he says, "Well, your lodgings are free, and you'll get £11 a week. Start at eight o'clock on a Monday morning, and you're back home on Friday at five o'clock. Off Saturday and Sunday." That was unbelievable! So, I took the job.'

– *Bobby Clark*

On their living conditions

'We got the union rate, whatever the union rate was. When I started as a first-year apprentice, I think it was about £1/12/6d for a week. But, of course, we had the other considerable bonus of having our keep as well. The keep was part of the contract really. And we were very, very well looked after. The food was excellent, and we had all our home comforts.'
– *Hugh Lamont*

'Oh, I should tell you about the craftsmen's mealtimes. The craftsmen and their labourers started their work immediately after the morning service at eight, and they went on and did what they were instructed to do until about nine-ish – and up they come! Big hunks of bread, spread with jam, were demolished along with cups of tea. And then they came in to lunch, and that was a proper dinner. So that was a substantial meal. And then, in the afternoon, it would be another small break for tea, and then the evening meal. And for the evening meal, the young minister men had to dress in their navy blue shirts, their suits and ties – no mucky overalls. So it was more formal then. The other meals were less formal, but there was always Grace before, and "Thank You" afterwards, before we left the tables.'
– *Laura Mathers*

'We lived in the huts in front of the Abbey. They stretched along the east front of the Abbey, and led up to a common room, kitchen, bath, toilet, and rooms, with a big room at each end. Calum Macpherson, in later years, got one to himself – he was the foreman. I think Dr MacLeod used the other one at times. Well, you could hear him at about one in the morning tramping away down, when he'd been workin' late.'
– *Adam Campbell*

'We all had separate rooms. They were very good, and very comfortable. You couldn't ask for better. Calum put me next door to him, that was the boss, and I used to always have the wireless on. And every time the wireless was on, he used to knock at the door about twelve o'clock, and say, "Get these girls out your room!" And I would shout

back, "It's the wireless!" One time though, the big knock comes, "Would you get that wireless off, Bob?" And that's the only time I had a girl in the room!'
– *Bobby Clark*

'I think there was quite a sense of loss when the huts were removed, because it had a great atmosphere about it that place. And the common room where we dined, it was all windows right across that front side, and you looked out across the Sound to Mull, and it's a marvellous view that, especially in the evening when you're sitting at your tea, and the sun's shining on the red granite along the south end of Mull. So peaceful as well. There wouldn't be a sound, apart from the corncrakes[24] in the St Columba Hotel field.'
– *Hugh Lamont*

On the work

'You had the ministers labouring to you at certain times, and then they went to study. The first year, we had a bit to do to the Chapter House.[25] The roof had to be done, and that was built. But, at the same time, we were busy unloading boats with beds, divans and desks, and that. And cement. And some stone. So that was our first bit of action.'
– *Adam Campbell*

'The puffer would come and anchor in Martyrs' Bay. It would come in at high tide and beach itself, and wait till the tide went down. So, if the low tide happened to be at midnight, or in the middle of the night, everybody was down with their horses and carts, or whatever they had, to get their ration of coal or whatever, because it had all been ordered. So the green lorry was pressed into service for this, and you went down, and the hold was emptied, scoopful by scoopful of whatever it was, and driven up to the Abbey. And the green lorry was tipped at the back of the dyke behind Tor Abb.[26] So there was a big heap of coke, a big heap of anthracite, and a huge heap of coal as well. And all that then, of course, had to be carried in buckets down to the boiler house.'
– *Laura Mathers*

'At the end of the year in 1939, there were call-ups, and you could see folk drifting away to register. In 1940, they got permission to build, because they were only using lime and granite. It wasnae interfering with the war effort. And there was old boys there, too old for the army, or men waitin' to register. The Ministry of Works said, "It's okay. You can build." Carts would go down onto the beach, to the high-water, and took about a hundredweight of sand up with the horse. It was taken up to the Abbey and put into these tubs in the cloisters where the rainwater washed it – took out any salt. Now, I think, it has to be imported, the sand. In 1940, we built the refectory and the gable, and it was all ready to roof – which happened after the war, in 1948. But I joined the Air Force after that, though there was two or three masons exempt [from war service] that worked up there during the war.'

– Adam Campbell

'There was no electricity on the island. We were working with the light of Tilley lamps – pressure lamps – all the time. And in the wintertime, of course, we had them with us, more or less, all day. All the work was done entirely by hand. I think probably the most important point, from a joiner's point of view, is the preparation of the timber. I mean, the only power tool that we had there was a petrol-driven circular saw. So once the timber went through the saw, everything from that point was done by hand. And, of course, it meant that any timber that had to be planed had got to be planed by hand. And size didn't make any difference – whether it was small pieces or large pieces, they had all got to be planed by hand. I can recall when we made a lot of the sliding-sash windows for the East Range. There's so many different components go into the making of a sliding-sash window: many different sizes, and different shapes, and all this stuff was planed by hand. I remember doing nothing but planing timber from morning to night, literally, for weeks on end.'

– Hugh Lamont

'We had to get the wood from somewhere, and timber then, of course, was all under licence. You had to get a licence, and a special permit, so they decided that they would get salvaged wood. The wood that we

used was actually jettisoned cargo from a Canadian ship that was washed ashore on Mull. Of course, being in the water, some of it had oil and all sorts of things on it. It wasn't nice, clean, bright timber. The first roof was the reredorter,[27] and I really enjoyed it. The following year, they got this Norwegian wood. It was nice and clean. Fresh to work with.'
– *John Young*

'Quite a lot of the wood came in gifts really – the likes of the timber for the refectory: that was a gift from the Norwegian government. Dr MacLeod went and pointed out to the Norwegians the devastation that the Vikings had caused in the past, and it was about time they made some kind of reparation! A lot of the timber for the East Range came from Australia. Exactly what the circumstances of that gift were I'm not quite sure, because they were just finishing off part of it when I went there. The timber for the cloisters – that was all Canadian red cedar. That was a gift from Canada.

When we were restoring the cloisters, the large beams which support the roof of the cloisters all had to be planed by hand, every one of them. We checked roughly how much there was, and there was something in the region of three hundred feet of these beams, and they were ten inches wide and six inches thick, and they were in varying lengths. We used the longest beam to start off with, and that was all Canadian red cedar, and this was a ten-by-six beam – ten-inch by six-inch – and it was twenty-seven feet long! And I planed all that up by hand, myself. It was just planed on two sides: one ten-inch face and a six-inch edge: the other side was against the wall, and the other edge was upwards, so it's not seen. That is quite an undertaking.

This was done just at the beginning of the summer, before the 'New Men' and the visitors started coming, but when they came, they were all organised to plane these beams. They were all people that we just taught to use planes. Oh, and they did sterling work, there was no doubt about that. They did what you might refer to as the "donkey work": they took all the roughness off all those beams. But, of course, they weren't particularly expert in the use of the plane, so the finished

quality of the planing wasn't good enough for the job. So, after they'd finished with them, I'd to go over every one of them with the steel plane, to get rid of all the plane marks, and that sort of thing. So, in a way, I more or less planed up all the three hundred feet of that ten-by-six!'
– *Hugh Lamont*

'The trusses for the refectory roof were made to a certain template, and we mapped out all the various joints – everything was done by hand, no machinery – and we made all these trusses on the ground, and made a ramp up to the wall-head of the refectory, and put the trusses up, one by one, with the aid of twelve of the ministers lifting each piece up, one by one.

So we got the roof trusses up, but by this time, the winter was coming on, so we managed to get the covering on the roof. That was flooring boards, rather than sarking boards. And we were able to get scaffolding inside the refectory, and we worked up there during the winter with the light of Tilley lamps. It was quite a dangerous exercise. In fact, at one point, Adam Campbell slipped from one of the scaffolding levels onto the one below. Had he not caught onto another piece of wood, he would have fallen all the way down to the ground. So it had its element of danger in it.

We got the framework up for the barrel roof. And we had a man up from the *Scots Magazine*, and he spoke to us and took pictures, and that item was published in 1948 or 1949, and it showed Campbell and myself working with specially shaped hand-tools, hand-planes, for the shape of the roof. It was very hard physical work.

Iain Lindsay, he was the architect from Edinburgh, and he kept a very close watch on it, both on the stonework side of it and on the woodwork side. And when the time came to do the slating – the slates were three feet long by an inch-and-a-half thick – the slating was done by slaters from Oban who worked there for quite some time. Very heavy work again, of course.

When you have no machinery, you've got to know what you're doing. In those days, my job was to sharpen hand-saws three days a week, because I was the only one who could do that from my training in the shop where I learned my trade. We did have a motorised saw, but it kept breaking down. Any time you tried to put wood through, it would just cut out. So my job, latterly, was to sharpen all the saws, and keep them in good order. And the others worked away, while I sharpened the tools.'

– *Joe Blair*

'I remember the stone mason who was there was Bill Amos. We used to try and persuade him to climb up the side of the wall, because he was a super climber, as well as a super stonemason. But he was the kind of person that didn't like to show off, or anything like that. And I learned quite a lot from him. I learned how to split stones, and how to dress them, and everything. And that stood me in good stead, because I became Head of a building department, and I had stone masons in the department.'

– *John Young*

'The stone that came from Fionnphort to do the West Range was from the two old ferryman's houses that went on fire, and burnt down. So the Abbey enquired about it, and they got it for the West Range. And then there was a boat gifted from Ireland – "The Derry" – and there was a man, MacPhail, who was a nephew of the MacPhails who live on Iona – he was the skipper of it. And it was all shipped over – carried, by hand, into the boat, and over to Iona.

Oh, it was a big job. It was a big, big heap. And when it landed up in the Abbey, it was just in one massive pile. When I looked around with the mason for stone, I didn't need to hunt for any: he would come along, and he would just point, "That one. That one. That one. That one." They never measured them: they just looked at them. And you just took the stones, rolled them up a plank, and within half-an-hour to an hour, they had a line of stone up, without chipping it or anything. They just fitted. Oh, they were very professional masons. It was hard work, heavy work, but we could handle it. And I'm very proud of the building, because it's a beautiful building. Beautiful.'

– *Bobby Clark*

'The very last job that I did before I left was to make the Communion table that stands in the Michael Chapel.[28] The ceiling in there as well, of course – it's that curved ceiling – it's made from that African utile, and that was quite a special job as well, it being curved. And the boards were all random widths. It was a big job that. It was certainly a very satisfying piece of work, that's for sure. It's nice to go in, and have a look at it.'

– Hugh Lamont

On their employer

'George MacLeod was a very, very forceful personality. When he walked into a room, you realised that he'd arrived. And he was a big man. He was an imposing-looking figure, and he was a very imposing personality as well. He was a man who could stamp his personality on any sort of gathering, really.'

– Hugh Lamont

'Well, he was imperious, of course, being an army man, and you expected that. If he wanted something done, you said, "Yes! Yes!" And then worried about how to do it afterwards.'

– Laura Mathers

'When George MacLeod was on-site, the day started rather dramatically. He told us the night before that he would be swimming in the Sound of Iona, and he expected us all to be there. We went down there at six o'clock in the morning with our towels, but George was wrapped round with a huge shawl which had been made for him by the people in Mull, and he said, "I'm going in, and the rest of you will follow me." So he threw off this shawl, and he had not a stitch on underneath. And he ran, and jumped in the water, and, as he jumped in, his body went into the water and you could see him turning, and he was almost running before his feet hit the ground. He was out first, the shawl wrapped round his body. "Right, all of you, get in!" We were all frozen by the time we got back out of there.'

– Joe Blair

'He managed the tradesmen. He didn't talk you down or that, but when we went there, he said, "Now, call me Boss." So, instead of "Dr MacLeod this", or "Dr MacLeod that", it was "Boss".'
– *Adam Campbell*

'Dr George MacLeod, he was the boss, and he was one of the best bosses I ever worked for. I was in Nairn Construction, and I'm telling you, they were nothing to Dr George. He came once a month, and he took us, one at a time, up to his house, Dunsmeorach, and he asked if you'd got any problem. "Is there anything you'd like changed?" Or, "Are you happy?" And then he took out his bottle of whisky – and beer – so you had a drink with him. And he was a pleasure to meet. And I think if a lot of bosses did the same, construction work would be much better.'
– *Bobby Clark*

'He was a born leader, but he was very caring. He was really good at getting everybody involved in things. I can remember, when we were staying in the library, he would come up at night and have a chat with us. Sometimes, I think he maybe used that as a way of trying out his sermon. But there's nothing wrong with that. Or maybe trying out some of his ideas. As far as I was concerned, it was an illustration that everybody meant something to him, and I thought that was very, very important. I had a lot of respect for him.'
– *John Young*

On the ministers

'We got on fine after a bit. We got pally with some – well, I got pally with Graham Bailey. Kept in touch with him even when he was abroad and I was abroad, and we kept in touch ever since. We got on fine with Uist and "Big Mac" – big Hamish MacIntyre. Big chap. Heavy-set. We were in the puffer once [shovelling coal], and the skipper was quite impressed with him. Wouldnae believe he was a minister. He said, "Ach well, if he cannae get a kirk, he can get a job with me."'
– *Adam Campbell*

'There was John Harvey, Maxwell Craig, and a Mr Graham. And their job was to come to the shore with me and load up the lorry with gravel. And they were very good workers. They'd get a job in construction work any day. Yes, great workers. And we had a good time.'
– *Bobby Clark*

'Obviously, they weren't skilled men, but there was so much that had to be done that didn't particularly require the skill of tradesmen: things like hauling sand from the machair. These were jobs that could be very time-consuming if the craftsmen had to be taken off their work to do it, whereas we had all that extra help throughout the summer. I think we were all a little bit sorry to see them go when the summer came to an end, because they all integrated very well with the craftsmen. And it was, I suppose, a real sense of community living with them. By the end of the summer, when you'd been working with these people, and living with them for so long, obviously friendships did develop, but, once they were gone, that tended to be it. I don't think there was much in the way of personal contact kept up. But it was always nice to see them coming back the following year.'
– *Hugh Lamont*

'Well, they learned quite quickly the small tasks they had to do. Bob Craig[29] and I cut most of the main beams of the roof and, of course, the beams being fifteen inches wide, the mortise and tenon joints[30] were a third of that – five inches. We had muscles like Charles Atlas, of course, by the time we were finished. The smaller trusses we allowed the ministers to maybe bore. We had auger bits[31] – one-and-a-half-inch to two-and-a-half-inch auger bits to bore through at an angle, because the roof was very steep. All the mortises were at an angle, so it took a long time. I'm quite sure that when the ministers went back to the parishes, they would have had muscles like nobody's business.'
– *Joe Blair*

'We got permission, through the Church of Scotland, to work the glebe at the manse, and some of the young ministers went out to cultivate it. They had a cart with a donkey, "Nebo". If I mind right, it had to work every second day, and I think the beast knew it, because it was

stabled in one of the ruins, and it would get out of there easy enough, and away up the road, braying, "Hee-haw, hee-haw." You heard it in the evening service in the summertime. The chap that took charge of the donkey was a minister – Marcus Barth. I think his father was a theologian.[32] But Marcus was the only one that could make it work.'
– *Adam Campbell*

On worship

'We had to go to the service at eight o'clock every morning. Well, you didn't have to go, but if you didn't go to the service, you had to start work at eight o'clock – you had to go to the site. So, naturally enough … Well, what would you do? I'd rather sit in church at the service than go to work. So everybody went.'
– *Bobby Clark*

'Oh, the impressive thing, as far as I was concerned, was that you were sitting in a choir stall with other craftsmen and the ministers. One of the things that appealed to me was one of the principles that they had, which was "Work is worship: labour, holy". I thought that was brilliant, and it gave the workmen a place in the Community. And you were doing that in the morning, before you started work, and then you were doing it later on in the evening. I cannot really remember the text or some of the things that were being spoken about, but just the whole feeling – and the fact that you were singing together with them without any accompaniment, for most of the time anyway. So it really was an experience, and to me it illustrated what a real community could be like. That was the important thing.'
– *John Young*

'Evening prayers was a wonderful experience. They had "laying on of hands", and George MacLeod would invite people to come forward to be recommitted, which most people did.'
– *Joe Blair*

'The Sunday night service at nine o'clock was like a Quaker service. It was silent, because Quakers, of course, sit at peace. And if you feel

that you wish to pray about anything in particular, you pray, either silently, or out loud, if you want other folk to know what you are praying about, and they pray with you. Or you're just quiet for fifteen minutes, until the leader says that that's the end. There's a benediction, and then you may go out and up to the refectory, of course, for your cocoa and buns.'
– *Laura Mathers*

On leisure

'We went on a boat trip to the lighthouse. You could just see it on the horizon. We were lucky. Usually you have to land with a breeches buoy, but the weather was calm, so we could land on the rock. But it wasn't much of an advantage, because the doorway was about thirty feet up, so you had a big vertical ladder to climb, and you were going up wi' your knees hittin' your chin. I was glad when I got to the top and somebody grabbed me in. But all the time we were going round, I was thinking of going down. But it was neat. The granite floor was all interlocked, and wee, minute hand-basins, curved to suit the wall.'
– *Adam Campbell*

'I walked the island along with John Kane and Adam Campbell. Every Sunday afternoon, we would walk round the island, and we watched the changing seasons: geese coming in to land, and storms.'
– *Joe Blair*

'One dinner time, in 1939, we were waiting on dinner in the common room. The common room had a piano at the far end, and then there were two doors: one led off to the kitchen, and one led off to the living quarters. There was a crowd round the piano, and Cameron Wallace was playing the piano, and the tradesmen and others were sitting at the table, when the kitchen door opened. Dr MacLeod appeared, and heard the piano. Cameron used to play jazzy tunes, so he instantly got his arm here. Then the other door opened, and big Hamish, big six-footer appeared, and instantly caught on to what was happening. So Dr George brought his hands down, and Hamish puts his hands on his right shoulder, and they sashayed down (you know

how some of these girls dance?) to the applause of everybody. Big men. Big hearts. And big legs.'
– *Adam Campbell*

'In the evening, we had our "tea", as it is known in Scotland, and, thereafter, there might have been a concert in the refectory. George MacLeod had his "Wee cock sparra", and we did "I'll give you five O" ["Green grow the rushes O"]. I would play the pipes, and Reggie Barrett-Ayres, the Director of Music at Aberdeen University, he was there, and his party piece was: "Give me the name of any modern tune – any tune at all – and I'll play it as Beethoven would play it." Usually something like "She'll be coming round the mountain".'
– *Joe Blair*

'I memorised all George MacLeod's party pieces: "A lum hat wantin' the croon", "The poor old lady she swallowed a fly"; and one of the Community members made up a song for us to sing. It was a parody on something else:

"We came here we thought to go building a roof.
Integrate. Integrate. Community …"

I cannae remember all the words of it …

"There was Archie McGavin, Leslie Dickie, Willie Paddell, John Young and Uncle James Bowman and all."

That was the chorus!'
– *John Young*

'In the summer, of course, there were always so many other attractions. We had the football match on a Wednesday night. I think it was probably myself that was instrumental in getting the football match organised. We got up a team at the Abbey composed of, well, whoever was available. And then there was a team got up between the village and the North End camp, and we played everybody on Wednesday night up in what's known as "Burnside Stadium". Oh, we had some wonderful matches up there. And then, of course, we had some

marvellous dances on a Tuesday night and a Friday night as well.'
– *Hugh Lamont*

'Oh, the village dances. They were wonderful. Friday night was dancing night. The village hall didn't have any toilet facilities in those
days, but it had a stage with curtains which didn't really work very
well, and there was this wonderful wind-up gramophone, with a very
few records of the old-fashioned kind – none of your 45s! They were
the old-fashioned 78s. So, somebody's job was to wind up the gramophone, and start the dance. They were very well-attended, and everybody who could, would cram into the hall. The dancing was Scottish
country dancing. Visitors who didn't know how to do it were soon
pulled round "Strip the Willow". The willow was stripped with regu-
larity, and eightsome reels were done in all sorts of directions. Those
who had country dancing lessons in their mainland places were often
shocked at the way that they were done, because the steps weren't
right. However, everybody was happy, and the dances went on until it
was dark. In the summertime, of course, it didn't get dark all that
much! When the gramophone started to get a bit slow, there was a
dash to the stage to wind it up again, and since the only modern
dancing thing was "Carolina Moon" and something else on the other
side, the ballroom-dancing-type dancing was not all that often. We
stuck with things like "Petronella", or "Strip the Willow", or "St
Valerie". So, they were very, very joyful occasions – noisy and joyful.'
– *Laura Mathers*

A high day

'The Queen's visit was 1956, and things were all go. I thought the
island was going to sink with folk coming over from Mull. The refectory was packed. I was introduced to the royal family as a Community
member, so I had my blue suit on. There was the Queen, Prince
Philip, Princess Margaret. We were interested in Margaret, because
that's when she gave up a boyfriend.[33] Nowadays, they talk about the
Prince's gaffes, but he never made any then. I thought he was very
sensible, because he was introduced to Calum, and said, "What bit
are you working on now? Have you got plans? No?" And he said to

John Kane, "Would you go and get them?" And what I liked about the Duke, then he said, "When that chap comes back, see that he comes, and doesn't get left hanging, so to speak." So John Kane came back, and he had a look at where we were working.'
– *Adam Campbell*

'Everything went like clockwork. Jessie and Ella and I were up making trifles all Friday and Saturday morning, then seeing that all was tidy, not forgetting the bathroom. On Sunday morning, it was breakfast at seven-thirty, working party muster eight o'clock, then everyone was flying round: Lindsay Robertson scrubbed the kitchen floor for Mary. I was in with ham and salad: I had ninety-five done, before we went down to get dressed for the Abbey. Ursula MacLeod and I sat together. I had on my navy dress and light cardigan, and my pearls. When the party came in, Alex [Barbara's husband][34] had to go up and meet them, and bring them down. He didn't think he was just in front of the Queen – he thought all the ministers were coming down first – but when he came inside, there was Charles Warr,[35] then the Queen and the Duke, then Princess Margaret, and then Dr MacLeod and all the ladies-in-waiting, etc. She looked very nice. Both her and Margaret were very plainly dressed and not much make-up. Dr MacLeod preached great. The Duke read the lesson. They went into the north transept after the service, which looks good, then up the night stairs. Ursula MacLeod and I were let out of a side door, so that we could get up to the kitchen, and Alex was there waiting. HM stopped at the old library, and met the members of the Session, then looked into a room with new furniture, and one with old. Then came to the kitchen. We had been told to stand in the wash-up part. She came in and looked at the stove, and then turned round, and Alex was presented first, then me, and then Ursula. She was very nice. She asked Alex how long he'd been here, and then asked me if I liked to live on the island, and was it lonely in winter? How many had we staying? And then Princess Margaret came up, and we were presented to her, and she talked a while. Then the Queen shook hands with us again, and wished us, "Good morning", and then it was Margaret's turn. They went into the refectory, where Jessie, Ella and Tom, and also the Pratts, had seats, and she met Jenny and Ralph [Morton], also Lady MacLeod, John Kane, Adam [Campbell], and Calum [Macpherson]. Then down to the Chapter House where the Trustees were. Then Mr Lindsay [the Project architect] took her round the Abbey and cloisters, etc, with George [MacLeod] and the Duke in great form together. Then she met Morag [MacPhail, the post-mistress], Mrs MacArthur [the school teacher], old Betsy [a crofter], and, after leaving the Abbey, she came down to the Relig Odhráin. Mary and Max MacLeod gave her a St John and a St Martin's cross for Prince Charles and Princess Anne, and Max had a good bit talk to her. And when he bowed, we thought he was going to stay bent all day. She went into the nunnery, and we were all to the jetty to see her off.'

Extract from a letter from Barbara Hislop to her son, Joe, and daughter-in-law, Joan, August 1956

A dark day

'It was 1955.

The puffers – flat-bottomed boats – used to bring coal to the islands. They come in onto the beach at high tide, and then, when the tide goes out, the tractors come alongside, and the coal is unloaded that way. And the same was being done with the timber that came into Martyrs' Bay, which is where the puffers normally come in.

Charlie Kirkpatrick and myself were in the hold, making up the slings for the timber. We'd been working all day, and we got to the point where it was the very last sling of timber to go out. It was those beams, supporting the roof of the cloisters. They were the last pieces to go out. We made up this sling of timber, and the two slings that we'd put on, they wouldn't quite meet in the middle, to hook onto the crane that was hoisting them out. So Charlie and I were on one side of what was quite a pile of timber, and there was another spare sling on the other side of the hold. So Charlie says to me: "Come on, you're the youngest. Climb over, and get that sling." So I went over and got the sling, and we threaded it through the two slings that were already on, and then onto the crane, and, naturally, I stood back to that side – the side I was on. And, of course, Charlie stayed where he was. And they were hoisting it up.

The chap who was operating the crane couldn't see into the hold, so he'd got someone up on the deck who was indicating to him. I mean, there are a properly-recognised series of hand-signals that's used for conveying the message to the chap who's operating the crane, whether to raise, or lower, or what to do.

However, as this timber was going up, one of these long lengths of timber caught just under the edge of the hold, and before the chap who was giving the signals could convey to the chap who was operating the crane to stop hoisting, it got to the point where the strain got too much for the sling – for this one sling it was on – and it broke, and the timber fell back ......

...... Anyway the timber fell back, and, fortunately, I had stood back to the side that I was on, but the timber was going out of the other side of the hold, and when it fell back, Charlie was just these few vital inches too far forward, and the timber just caught him a glancing blow. It didn't land on top of him. It must have just hit him on the head on the way down, and ...... it killed him outright on the spot ......

When ...... the timbers hit the floor, the sling ...... burst open, and it knocked me back against the side of the boat, and ...... of course, I thought the same had happened to Charlie, but ...... when I picked myself up, he was ...... still lying on the other side and ...... we found that it had killed him, there and then.

And then, of course, there was a Court of Enquiry in Oban, which we had to attend ...... And Charlie's children were all very young ...... he had four children ...... the oldest I think was about seven years old ...... So it really was a terrible tragedy ...... and it left its mark for quite some time I think ...... particularly on us who were working there ...... but I would imagine on the Community as a whole ...... I know I went home that day ...... I can't remember exactly what day of the week it was that it happened, but I know I was ...... sent home, and I was at home for a few days ...... That actual part of it ...... immediately after the accident ...... it's something that ...... didn't really register in my mind. I don't really remember much about that ……… I remember the accident itself, and … the detail …… but what happened …… the rest of that day, or that night, or shortly after it … I couldn't tell you much about it, to be quite honest ……

I mean it all happens in a split second, doesn't it? It's just over before you realise … what's happening … It was … a bigger tragedy for his family than it was for us, of course …… but it was a shock to the whole island ……'

– *Hugh Lamont*

On the lasting influence of Iona

'It was very influential in my life, and Isobel, my wife, and I talk about it often. Iona was a focal point for many things. A springboard. My work on Iona was very much of a practical nature, but the longer I stayed on Iona, the more interested I became, not just in the practicalities of my work, but in the work of the Church. And I also met my wife on Iona.'

– *Joe Blair*

'I think that the experience built up my confidence in my own abilities. I mean, I was doing odd jobs that none of the rest of the group could do, so I was earning the name as a sort of "Mr Fix-it". And, at fifteen, it was a big boost.'

– *John Young*

'What we were doing ourselves on the rebuilding – that was important to me. I always looked on that as something very special, and I always consider myself to have been very privileged to have been the only apprentice that worked on the Abbey.'

– *Hugh Lamont*

'One of the things that I was really happy about was receiving a Bible. It's marked "In friendship. Iona, 1944". And there's a list of people in it: George MacLeod, Lex Miller, Bill Amos, Grant Anderson, James Currie, Douglas Trotter, Colin Day, Charles Forman, Johnnie MacMillan, Robin Service, Dinah Fallon (who was one of the cooks), Mary

Hamilton (another cook), and George – McMeekin, is it?

And at the bottom there's a prayer that George MacLeod put in, and I thought that was interesting, being a joiner myself:

O Jesus, Master Carpenter,
Who, at the end, through the wood and nails of the cross
Did purchase Man's salvation,
Wield well thy tools within our life
That we, who come rough-hewn,
May be, by thy hand,
Fashioned to a finer beauty. Amen.'
– *John Young*

'Well, it has been a source of comfort, I suppose, in the sense of "comfort" in the Latin, which means "with strength". Something to give you strength through all kinds of things that happened afterwards. Because everything we did, and everywhere we went to work after that, we were always able to be in touch with other people who knew about Iona. You were just an extended family in a kind of a way.

Oh, that I could live for ever
over the Sound of Iona.
I would leave thee never, never,
beautiful Sound of Iona.
Sail away, sail away
over the Sound of Iona.'[36]
– *Laura Mathers*

1

2

5

6

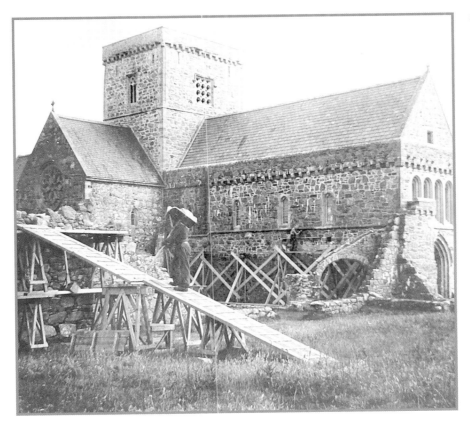

9

10

Photos

1. George MacLeod provided accommodation for both the craftsmen and the ministers in the huts (Raymond Bailey archive)

2. Left to right: Bill Amos, Adam Campbell and Calum Macpherson (Joe Blair archive)

3. Joe Blair (centre) arriving on Iona for the first time (Joe Blair archive)

4. The Common Room of the 'Rome Express' (Calthorpe Emslie archive)

5. The puffer anchored in Martyrs' Bay (Faith Aitken archive)

6. The Norwegian wood is delivered by the puffer (Faith Aitken archive)

7. The Community lorry transfers goods from the jetty to the Abbey (Duncan Finlayson archive)

8. Stones were carried or rolled up the ramp (Raymond Bailey archive)

9. Minister Bob Craig and craftsman Joe Blair prepare the roof ties (Joe Blair archive)

10. Only Marcus Barth could control 'Nebo', the donkey (Raymond Bailey archive)

11. The Queen's visit to Iona, 1956 (Molly Harvey archive)

12. Alex and Barbara Hislop (Joe Hislop archive)

The Community and work

As far as the young ministers who joined the Community were concerned, George MacLeod's experiment in theological education was a success. They came to Iona, experienced manual labour, often for the first time, got to know working men, again, often for the first time, and were changed by that experience. The assessment of Graeme Brown, who joined the Community in 1960, is typical:

'George MacLeod believed that if he could get the young ministers to come and actually share in the building work with the craftsmen, they would find a new vision of what the responsibility of the Church was. And it happened. We went up there as new members, and got a new vision.'
– *Graeme Brown*

What is equally clear, however, is that there was then an enormous range of responses to the insights gained during the time those young ministers spent rebuilding the Abbey. The baseline response was to opt to serve in an industrial parish:

'The Community persuaded us that the thing to do was learn our theology, do some hard physical work, know what it was like to labour, and go into an industrial situation, and labour there. In other words, not a posh parish.'
– *Ian Renton*

Some, like David Levison who found himself in Gorebridge where mining was the chief industry, simply used their experience on Iona to build relationships with the working men in their parish:

'I sometimes wondered if I wasn't wasting their time, going down and taking them away from their work just to chat to them. But I found it, for myself, very enriching. Quite a number of my Kirk Session were miners. My Session Clerk was a miner. I don't think I got very far, but I felt I was extending the mission of the Church a little.'
– *David Levison*

Others combined parish ministry with part-time industrial chaplaincy:

'I had hoped to do Church Extension work, but Penry Jones, who was the Industrial Secretary, and Maxwell Craig [another member of the Community] were elders in St Mark's Church in Greenwich, and they leaned on me to come as minister there. And, of course, it was an industrial parish. I was Chaplain, among other things, to three industries in Greenwich and Woolwich. Not a paid job, but just because the Community had said this is what you should be doing. So the Community gave me a total incentive to labour in an industrial situation.'
– *Ian Renton*

Still others, like George Wilkie and Ian Fraser, believed that industry itself might be their parish:

'Harry Whitley, who had been with George MacLeod in Govan, went down to Port Glasgow. It was the lower reaches of the Clyde shipbuilding, and he was very friendly with Sir James Lithgow who was the owner of the shipyards there. And he said to me, "I'll get Sir James to put up some money for you, and make you a chaplain in the shipyards." Now, I wasn't very sure about this. However, I accepted it, and for a couple of years I was a chaplain in the shipyards. It was a marvellous experience really, with access to any yard I wanted to go into on the lower reaches, running groups, and discussions, and conferences, and so on.'
– *George Wilkie*

George Wilkie also provides a unique insight into the kind of project that the Community's Industrial Chaplains developed. With the help of Oliver Wilkinson, the Community's Drama Specialist, he produced a play which was conceived, written and performed by the people who lived and worked in Port Glasgow. Oliver Wilkinson had pioneered Community Drama in the 1940s, as a means of empowering poor communities. He encouraged them to take the raw materials of their own lives, and write about them:

'For a whole year, he had a group of shipyard workers and managers talking about it, and, in the end, when I arrived in 1948, they had a

script. And they had all contributed to it. It was a great thing for me, because it was the story of the Port. It was all about a young boy who had come to the Port just before the war, and the war experience, and about a family, and how they lived.'
– *George Wilkie*

Although George Wilkie moved on to more conventional parish ministry, this short-term experience of industrial chaplaincy was to have a long-term influence on him. The valuing of working people's insights would remain central to his ministry:

'I had actually just ten weeks to wait while I was waiting on the parish. And so I went to one of the managers of the Greenock Dockyard, and said, "Would you give me a job for ten weeks? I've got no work." So he says, "I'll put you in the light squad – the labourers." And so for ten weeks, I worked in the shipyard as a labourer, and I think that that helped. But I wouldn't have done that if I hadn't been a member of the Community. And people used to say to me, "Of course, you'll know, Mr Wilkie. You've been in the yards." Of course, it wasn't real. It was a bit of experience, but not the pressure that was on these men. But after what I'd done though, I did run the industrial side of things in the Presbytery, and had various conferences, and meetings with them.

I also started a Christian Workers' League which was quite important in the parish. These were Iona insights without a doubt.'
– *George Wilkie*

Ian Fraser also found himself working as a labourer, but not just for ten weeks. The understandings he had gained from his time working with the craftsmen on the Abbey led him to adopt a more radical model of chaplaincy. In the early 1940s, Ian became Industrial Chaplain in the Tullis Russell Works – a paper-mill in Markinch, in Fife – working full-time as a labourer:

'I was terrified – and determined! I remember standing looking into this hollow in which there were twelve hundred men. Okay, there were a handful of women, but it was really a male show, and I took my legs and made myself walk in that direction.

I found it was a place where it was very natural to go into a labouring gang, because the folk who were thought of as possible future managers or top administrators were made to see the work from the bottom, in every department. So there weren't any eyebrows raised when I was attached to a gang. But about ten days in, there was consternation. Two men came up and apologised for swearing in my presence: then I knew the cat was out of the bag! You see, I didn't know what to do. If I'd said, "I'm a minister", they might have thought I wanted special respect and status. If I didn't, they might think I was spying. You just work away until the thing becomes clear. And, well, I just had to pray my way through, and act as naturally as possible.

And then what happened was that the people got word to the next Section to which I was going, saying, "The minister will be with you next week, but he's all right." That's the best theological statement you could get: "He's all right." Because that meant you could just come alongside. One of the men might say to me, "The wife would like to meet you. Would you like to come up for a meal?" Or maybe, "My wife and I are having an awful job. We don't know how to work it out. Could you help a wee bit?" The best thing was relationship.'
– *Ian Fraser*

And although Ian did lead worship in the mill, it was not his top priority:

'On the Sundays, I took services of about twenty minutes, when folk who were on Maintenance had breaks. But I was always making clear that the taking of services was less important than being among the men, and doing the work. By the way, I could lift two-hundredweight loads. I just did exactly the same work as anybody else in the labouring, and I had just enough physical strength to do that.'
– *Ian Fraser*

So how did Ian judge the success, or otherwise, of this form of chaplaincy?

'Two years on, there was to be an assessment by me, and by the management, of whether the experiment should continue. My assessment was that if I were given another year, there were twelve people – only one of whom was a churchman – who could be left to be a heart of Christian perception in the mill, and I could move on to another industrial place, and start again. But I was told that the management had decided that, since I interfered in management decisions, they were not prepared – they were unanimously unprepared – to go ahead with the experiment, and I was thrown out. Not literally! I was given the chance to stay for a month or two, to find something else, but I was cut off.'

– Ian Fraser

To Ian, it felt like a terrible injustice at the time, but, with hindsight, did he feel that the management had a point? Had he interfered?

'I had, on two occasions, taken up questions of injustice. I'd taken them up directly with the management.'

– Ian Fraser

Certainly it would be no surprise if an Industrial Chaplain had been an irritant to management, but recently, Ian discovered what really led to his experiment being brought to an abrupt halt, 60 years previously:

'I got a phone call about six years ago from the Managing Engineer. He said, "It's high time I phoned you and told you this. Actually, the management team wanted the experiment to continue. But the chap who was called the Secretary, said to them, 'You will all unanimously agree to finish this experiment – or else!'" So I had that rough, and highly instructive, experience.'

– Ian Fraser

Although his own experiment in industrial chaplaincy had come to an end, Ian passed on the insights he had gained:

'Joe Oldham[37] asked me to provide a supplement for the *Christian Newsletter* in 1943, reflecting on the first year of working alongside people. And I think it probably did lead to the development of Industrial Mission, although I thought that you needed to work alongside people, accepting their conditions. I went in on a labourer's wage. It was very much the same as a Probationer's stipend in the Church of Scotland, but I think it did matter to be identified in that kind of way. There were folk who said to me, "You're really doing something marvellous. You're expressing solidarity with working people." No, I wasn't. I said, "I'm not. I've got degrees. I've got exits. But the folk here have nothing that they can earn money with, except this industry."

And then there were others who said, "You've let us down. You were supposed to be trained as a parish minister. You're supposed to be one of our theological educators, and you've gone into industry. You've just turned your back on it." And I said then in that supplement for the *Christian Newsletter*: "This is not a rejection of ministry, but a search for authentic ministry. This is not a rejection of theology, but a search for relevant theology. This is not a rejection of scholarship, but its completion."'
– *Ian Fraser*

Although Ian moved on in 1944, he too took many of the things he'd learned from his experience of chaplaincy into the next phase of his life as a parish minister:

'When we were in Rosyth, where I was minister for twelve years, the Kirk Session came one day, triumphantly, to me, and they said, "We've been meeting without you, and we've decided to raise your salary." And I said, "That's very gracious of you, but I'm afraid you haven't decided that. You have decided to *offer* me a rise in salary. I know that there have been increases in the dockyard wages, but my wife and I are not prepared to live above the level that's open to the rest of you in this community, so we'll have a discussion together about whether it would be a fair thing to take the additional income." And we decided it was fair – but only when we'd gone into the wages in the dockyard. But it certainly took them aback to hear that you don't simply accept a rise.'
– *Ian Fraser*

In addition to George Wilkie and Ian Fraser, there were many in the Community who were committed to finding new ways of relating to people in their workplace. Douglas Alexander is a former Warden of Community House, in Glasgow:

'The development of chaplaincies – industrial chaplaincy, of course – but indeed, the whole notion of chaplaincy – was nourished in Community House. And the Church took that whole strand of thinking to itself, and developed it further. Eventually we had hospital chaplaincies, and retail chaplaincies, and so on.'
– *Douglas Alexander*

The Glasgow headquarters of the Community, like Iona itself, was a hothouse of creative and radical thinking, and one of the people there who was most influential in industrial matters was Penry Jones.

Jim Wilkie, who would later join the Community, first encountered Penry when he was an undergraduate:

'I went up to university in Aberdeen in 1952, and was swept into the Student Christian Movement. At the end of the first year, I was looking for a holiday job – and one of the people who had been in the SCM a long time said there was this chap, Penry Jones, who was looking for students to go and be part of what he called a "Student Work Community" in Glasgow. It would consist of two and a half months of work. There would be a month in Glasgow, working in industry, and Jones would place us there. There would be a fortnight on this place called Iona, during the Glasgow Fair Fortnight. And then we'd go back for another month in the factory. So I set off for Glasgow, and when I got there, I found there were about eight or ten of us, and Penry was a kind of "éminence grise" who hovered over the whole affair, and who had great respect as a result.

So the plan was: get up in the morning, say prayers before breakfast, have some breakfast, and then go off to your work. Come back in the evening, and have some kind of activity most nights. Sometimes we had community meetings. And then, into bed, worn out usually.

I was put to work in Colville's Clyde Ironworks. I spent the first wee while shovelling coke. The furnaces ran twenty-four hours, and the

coke was fed from a conveyor belt, and each furnace took what it needed. There was always some left at the end, so it fell off the conveyor belt – technically, into a lorry, but then the lorry wasn't always there, so it fell onto the floor. We shovelled it from there into the lorry, when the lorry arrived. It was a sort of soft job for a young man who was going to be a minister, but it was interesting, and it was my first experience of industrial work. It really was an eye-opener.'
– *Jim Wilkie*

Jim's time in Colville's was an eye-opener in many ways – not all of them positive – but he remembers one incident with real affection:

'The supervisor of the casual labourers was a very interesting brother called John Davie, who was obviously a self-educated working man who read voraciously. He knew I was a Classics student at the university. He came round one day, and saw me shovelling away at this coke – endless toil as it was. So he looked me up and down, and said, "Aye, laddie, you've got the task of Syphilis."[38] I sort of smiled, and nodded, and he passed on. But I've remembered it ever since, because it's beautiful. When I left, he gave me a copy of *The Essays of Ruskin*.'
– *Jim Wilkie*

Later, when the rebuilding of Iona Abbey was completed, Penry Jones's 'Work Placement Scheme' would form the basis of a more formal programme of work, centred on Community House in Glasgow. By then, Douglas Alexander was Warden:

'In the late 1960s – the whole great tradition of working with the craftsmen, and rebuilding – was done. Finished. So Community House then became the centre of an exciting development in the training of new members of the Iona Community.

Instead of going to the island for a whole summer, they came to Community House for approximately two months, with an intense two weeks at the end of it all, on the island, at the Abbey.

For the months of July and August, the new members had to work in real jobs. We had men working in the Rootes car factory in Linwood.

We had them working in the Belhaven Brewery in Glasgow. We had them working in a big plumbing firm, although I hate to think what excesses of plumbing they inflicted on the poor Glaswegians. We had them working as warehouse delivery people, filling up vans, and going between different warehouses. They spent the day at work, and then, in the evenings, we had a whole series of seminars and reflective sessions: the kind of thing that had been happening previously on Iona.'
– *Douglas Alexander*

So convinced was Douglas Alexander of the value of such work experience in the training of ministers, that he came up with a bold plan:

'It was from this experience that I, but much more importantly George MacLeod, developed the whole notion of now going back to use Iona in a different way from previously: to use Iona, in close collaboration with Community House, for the training of ministers. Not just for new members of the Community, but for the training of ministers of the Church, and George MacLeod named this project "The Fifth Divinity College" – the four traditional ones in Scotland were St Andrews, Glasgow, Edinburgh and Aberdeen – but the Community decided that it did not want to go down that road.'
– *Douglas Alexander*

The truth was that, for some members, none of the Community's experiments with work had ever been radical enough. They had always been, to some extent, 'pretend' work. Some tasks, particularly towards the end of the rebuilding of the Abbey, had felt more like an exercise, than real, productive work:

'We actually knocked down a wall that had been built the year before – or built a wall that had been knocked down the year before. I can't remember! But, really, we were not engaged in any exciting rebuilding: we were, by George's diktat, out there labouring.'
– *Iain Whyte*

Some jobs had been specially arranged as favours to George MacLeod:

'The job [at the ironworks] had been negotiated by George from the

top. In other words, he'd spoken to the Chairman of the Board, and we were pushed in. So they had to find a job for me, basically.'
– *Jim Wilkie*

And always, as Ian Fraser described so eloquently, the ministers knew they could parachute out at any time. It wasn't that Ian Fraser, and others who shared his view, didn't understand the symbolic value of the rebuilding of the Abbey. They did. They just thought it didn't go far enough:

'The symbol was great, and the years that it took to bring the symbol into reality were very valuable. But I was a minister, and I was a labourer. I worked on the roads. I worked in ironworks. I worked in shipyards. George MacLeod never understood that.'
– *Walter Fyfe*

As Walter Fyfe sees it, George MacLeod was guilty of a failure of nerve: a reluctance to face up to the logical conclusion of his own convictions:

'George used to say that it wasn't just the ministers you had to look to. Not just the "Reverend Mr So and So", but the "Reverend Mr Such and Such, the plumber". He used to be full of phrases like this, but, in fact, he had no interest whatsoever in working life outside the Iona Community, in terms of the Spirit.'
– *Walter Fyfe*

For Walter, conventional models of chaplaincy would not do, because they were based on the premise that the chaplains were taking God out from the Church to the World. Walter firmly believed that God was already there:

'To me, spirituality came from my mates. I went to theological college, had all kinds of very interesting discussions on every aspect of theology, but never did I have anything so keen as, for year after year, I had in the hut, during the tea break, in the Highways Department, or in the shipyards.

People say, "Oh, these working-class people. They're all apathetic. They're not interested in politics. They're not interested in religion.

What can you do with them?" The point is they were far, far brighter
– far more interested. They accepted that I had been educated in a
way that they hadn't been able to be. They didn't resent that. But they
were interested in trying to pull out, "What's it all about then?" And
then contribute their part.'
– Walter Fyfe

Walter Fyfe believes that, while George MacLeod accurately identified
the problem – that the Church, as an institution, had nothing to say to
working people – he lacked the courage to acknowledge the corollary –
that working people had much to say to the Church:

'The squads were thrown together from all parts, but all the time that
I worked in labouring jobs, I never once found anybody rejected –
except one kind of person: that's the big-headed – but nobody else.
No matter what absurd things they did or backgrounds they had.
And, therefore, to them, the Church was very alien, because the
Church does the opposite. Pathetically, in spite of the fact that the
Church turns its back all the time, they still wanted, somehow, to
recognise it. But the Church has made itself so utterly, totally remote,
exclusive and in-turned, that it has no relevance at all.'
– Walter Fyfe

Interestingly, Walter allows for one noble exception:

'Community House was relevant, because there was a much wider
and more open-minded group of people meeting there. And if, at a
certain time in the day, there was a wee service held in the side chapel
in the dining room of Community House, people just got up and
went, had the service, and came out. That was fine.'
– Walter Fyfe

It's not surprising then that, feeling as he did, Walter moved on from the
Community to an even more radical experiment.

'First of all, you simply sensed the electricity. You can go to a concert, and people are, basically, snoozing. Or you can go to a concert, and the electricity sparkles, and everyone is on the edge of their seats. And George had that effect. He was a fantastic orator. And his prayers outshone any prayers I've ever heard anywhere. I think that was where he was a true genius, because that is where he became totally poetic.'
– *Ian Mackenzie*

Jack Kellet, who first experienced worship in the Abbey as a Youth Camper, still remembers the impact of George MacLeod's sermons:

'I remember, much later, when, to my surprise, I became a minister, trying to work out what it was about preaching that was different from teaching, or lecturing, or arguing. And when I looked back on George MacLeod's preaching in Iona Abbey, I became aware of a sense of awe that somehow arose about the place. It wasn't just convincing people of the rightness of a point of view or an understanding. It was a sense of being in the presence of God.'
– *Jack Kellet*

Of course, the danger inherent in having such a charismatic mentor was that the 'New Men' would fail to recognise the principles behind George MacLeod's worship and, when called upon to lead worship themselves, would simply imitate him. George Wilkie was a 'New Man' in the 1940s:

'We had the supreme leader of worship in George MacLeod, and it's really unfair to say that the worship, in anybody else's hands, would have been as great. I had to take worship three or four times during the summer, and it was very pedestrian stuff. But we all tried to follow George in some way. And that was the danger: that you weren't your-self! We tried to get the big phrase, and the thought, and so on – which was a good thing, as long as you didn't try to be George MacLeod!'
– *George Wilkie*

'It was normally George MacLeod on a Sunday, and Ralph Morton might help with the evening prayers sometimes, but it was the disci-ples, as it were, during the week. And it was very difficult not to half mimic George, because his language and his tone of voice were so

invasive, and persuasive. But I think they were pretty successful, the young guys, at doing "sincere" in their own language, but consistent enough with the kind of things that Ralph or George would do.'
– *Ian Mackenzie*

In retrospect, it's strange that George's use of 'the big phrase' was met with such universal approval, when it could so easily have alienated, as Ian Renton hints:

'I am ashamed to say it, but I cannot bear posh, eloquent preaching. Yet George spoke beautiful English, and his diction was perfect, and I don't think anyone has preached as well since in Scotland.'
– *Ian Renton*

So what was it that made George MacLeod's heightened, poetic language so acceptable to 'New Men' like Ian Renton, craftsmen, visitors and Youth Campers alike?

First and foremost, everyone acknowledged that it derived from an authentic Celtic heritage, even though they were equally adamant that the term 'Celtic' was never applied to Iona worship in the early years:

'The word "Celtic" never entered our conversation. It was never around.'
– *John Harvey*

But despite the fact that no-one remembers Community worship ever being labelled 'Celtic', many contend that the history of the island, and of the Abbey itself, imbued it with a special quality:

'The place was humming with Celtic mysticism. It has to do with Iona as a place, of course, because when you step onto the island, something does happen. You're "somewhere else", and "the thin place" is always a good description of it. And there was the sense of the past. Although George was incurably romantic about the past, and about Columba's monks, everybody felt it. You didn't have to be George to feel it.

And the second thing was the building itself, which was supremely successful at not getting in the way of that "thinness", because it was

also "thin". It's quite a thin building, compared with its length, and there are no baubles. It's just stone and plain windows. So the building, I think, had a humility and plainness which allowed all that in. As regards the worship itself, the challenge was, like the building, not to get in the way of all this.'
— *Ian Mackenzie*

And as far as the early members are concerned, George MacLeod certainly did not 'get in the way'. Indeed, there is a strong suggestion that George MacLeod's language and sensibilities were heavily influenced by the fact that he was, himself, a Celt.

First as a student, then as a member, Douglas Trotter worshipped regularly in the Abbey from 1938 onwards:

'George was a Celt. He didn't have second sight, but he was a Gael. A MacLeod. There's no good trying to put your finger on it, but this equipment he had – the way he put things – the way he preached – created a frisson in his listeners. And that's not a common thing: a once-seen, never forgotten kind of thing. That magnetism was part of his personal gift.'
— *Douglas Trotter*

'He was as dramatic as only the Celt can be. And he would raise you up with his voice to spiritual heights. And then chastise you at the same time! And he had this Celtic vibrancy about his prayers.'
— *Ian Renton*

'Worship in the Abbey was, for almost everybody who visited it, an overwhelming experience. I can still remember the hair bristling on the back of my neck at the sheer power of George MacLeod's prayers. When George took prayer in the Abbey, the walls of the ancient place shimmered, and, as he himself would put it, "they glowed red, the colour of blood". There was simply nowhere else in Scotland, at that time, where there was anything to compare with the power and with the "responsible mysticism" that characterised worship in the Abbey at that time. When George was leading prayer in the Service of Commitment for members of the Community, he would refer to

Patrick, and Ninian, and Martin, and Columba with us still. And, by God, you believed it! It was his Celtic characteristics, I suppose, coming out. But he really could convey that we live in this world, but, my goodness me, we also live in another world, if we could but see it, and hear it, and respond to it. With George, the Communion of Saints wasn't some dry doctrine: the Communion of Saints described a companionship that one could feel, and detect, and relish in the worship of the Abbey.'
– *Douglas Alexander*

George's son Maxwell also believes that his father was profoundly marked by his Gaelic heritage:

'I believe he was immensely influenced as a child by Gaelic tradition. He took me, half a dozen times perhaps, to introduce me to Gaelic people on Mull. And this is actually quite a Gaelic tradition: you take a child and leave them with somebody, maybe for two days. Farm them out in a different social environment. And he left me with two or three really, really old couples, where only Gaelic was spoken in the house. He loved the cadence in the speech. He loved the Gaelic obsession with the simple things in life. He really loved the Gaelic fascination with the great cycles of nature – if you look at his prayers, it's there again and again.'
– *Maxwell MacLeod*

No-one suggested, however, that leading worship came easily to George MacLeod. In fact, they acknowledged that it was the product of meticulous, hard work. While he may have tapped into natural gifts and sensibilities, it's clear that MacLeod worked at the content of his sermons and prayers in much the same way that a poet pares back ordinary prose to reach the very essence of meaning:

'Each sentence had a power of its own. And there was never a phrase which sounded as if it was pious "fill-in". Every word, every phrase, every sentence had its own strength of meaning.'
– *John Sim*

'Every word mattered. I don't know how much rewriting he did. I can

only guess. But it wasn't spontaneous. He didn't just get the gift of the gab. And that is why the people who went to these services never heard George as just spouting rhetoric.'
– *Ian Mackenzie*

And it seems that George MacLeod worked equally hard on the delivery of his prayers and sermons. Joyce Alexander lived with her family, for a time, in the Leader's house on Iona:

'George MacLeod's huge gift was his ability to take worship. And when we were on the Community staff and lived in Dunsmeorach, and George was there with you, you knew that that came out of the most incredible preparation. You would hear him at two in the morning, walking up and down his bedroom, practising his sermon! You couldn't get to sleep for it, and neither could the guests! There was brilliance there, but there was hard work as well.'
– *Joyce Alexander*

And an early encounter with George MacLeod helped Ian Mackenzie to understand the extent of that hard work:

'I'd heard him preach, and that was impressive enough, but at a university service in St Giles Cathedral, when I was editor of the student magazine, he preached a sermon which I thought was so topical, and so full of highly relevant ethical and political issues, that it would read perfectly well in the pages of the magazine. So I ran after him, and pulled his elbow, and explained who I was, and could I publish this? And with a nonchalance which completely took me by surprise, he took out of his little case a sheaf of papers, and gave them to me, and went off!

That was my first meeting with him, and also my first realisation of what a complex character he was, because, like an actor, every emphasis was in black and red ink. Almost every word in virtually every sentence was phrased, like a pianist or a conductor might phrase a piece of music, so that he got the exact moment of stress, at the right syllable. And when something was to be very loud, it was made very clear with red ink and underlinings.

I once saw a facsimile of a score of Sir Adrian Boult, the music conductor, who had a very clear philosophy of dynamics in a symphony. And George, I think, instinctively, but also with hard work – very hard work – crafted his sermons in that way.'
– *Ian Mackenzie*

And even late in his ministry, there is evidence of George MacLeod's application:

'When we first developed the Friday night Communions, George MacLeod decided that he would lead a Folk Communion. I was present, and it was, as George said, "a bit of a disaster", because George wouldn't have known what to do with a guitar. He would have danced to it, if someone else had played, but he wasn't your "happy-clappy" guitar kind at all. I can still remember he announced the song "Michael, row the boat ashore" as "MICHAEL ROW THE BOAT ASHORE". As if he was announcing "Ye gates, lift up your heads". The tone was just wrong.

But the point of this story is that the following Friday, George MacLeod said, "I'm taking this service again, because I've got to learn how to do it." That was part of the man's greatness. We're talking about this very distinguished preacher, recognising that he had still to learn all kinds of things. And on the second Friday night, people were crying with joy, and with release from tension, because of the incredible power of this Folk Service. It was just absolutely magic, because he'd sweated blood for a week, learning, or rather, unlearning, so much that he'd learned, in order to take this new, more experimental, more informal form of worship.'
– *Douglas Alexander*

But despite winning the wholehearted admiration of the people who actually worshipped on Iona, George MacLeod's leading of worship was met with outright hostility in other quarters.

By the 1940s, that period of particularly violent sectarianism which had erupted in Scotland in the 1920s was coming to an end, but its dying throes continued well into the second half of the 20th century. George's saying of the Creed, use of crafted, rather than extempore, prayers, and introduction of a weekly Communion were condemned as 'Romish' practices by many in the Church of Scotland, and by the Protestant establishment. But allegations that the Community was 'halfway to Rome' exasperated George MacLeod, as one 'New Man', Duncan Finlayson, remembers well:

'I can hear George's voice saying, "You know, what people in Scotland have to realise is that John Knox said the Creed every Sunday. Because this is what the Reformation was about – that people should know what they believed." Again, George MacLeod said, "John Knox had ordered prayers." He didn't think that people should just talk off the top of their head, which, in large areas of the Church of Scotland, was thought of as the correct thing to do. John Knox had a written liturgy with a place for impromptu prayer. And John Knox wanted to recover the Holy Communion for the people. After the Reformation, ministers were suspended in Scotland for celebrating Communion only twice a year! Now if you suggest we should have Communion every Sunday, or once a month, the average elder in many churches thinks that's Romish! The recovery of the Sacrament was one of the central things that George MacLeod was concerned about, and that related to the recovery also of the understanding and celebration of the Christian year.'
– *Duncan Finlayson*

But not only does Duncan Finlayson defend George MacLeod against the accusations of Romish practices, he is anxious to emphasise George MacLeod's reasons for re-introducing a structured liturgy:

'This was not recovering tradition for the sake of tradition, or saying which tradition is the one that you follow, but simply that this "spoke" to people. Young people responded to a more ordered worship that wasn't people just talking off the tops of their heads.

It's easy to forget why the Community came into existence – and that was George's concern for the people – the ordinary people of Scotland – who felt that the Church was "not for the likes of them". I worked in Bridgeton and in Anderston, two really desperate areas of human need, and the Church in places like Bridgeton had almost fled. But

George's concern was the downtown churches, and the downtown areas, and it is a well-known fact that ordered worship is one of the things that spoke to people in their desolation. They wanted the mystery. It's why the Roman Church had more to say to ordinary people. When they went in, they felt they were in the presence of a mystery, and not the kind of intellectual, or pseudo-intellectual thing that marked much of Presbyterian worship. What I'm really saying is that these other things that we're talking about are only relevant because they related to George's concern – that's to say, the church-less. I think it's terribly important to understand that George's concern was not for tidier worship, or richer worship, for its own sake – in a disembodied way. It was because of his passion for people.'
– *Duncan Finlayson*

George MacLeod's championing of a structured liturgy, it seems, was utterly in keeping with the driving motivation behind the founding of the Community itself.

Richard Holloway, who came to membership of the Community from an Episcopalian tradition, recognised, at once, MacLeod's integrity of purpose:

'I was trained in the Anglo-Catholic style of Anglicanism which had brought a lot of colour, and lights, and mystery back into worship. But alongside that had always gone a commitment to social action. In other words, the transcendence had to be incarnated – had to be made immanent in actual, practical, political, human situations. The idea was that if you simply had action without worship, you lost the vertical aspect; if you simply had worship without action, you lost the horizontal aspect. So, the ideal combination – the complete package, as it were – was mystery, worship, transcendence, co-active with political engagement.

I remember one of the things that George MacLeod was always quoting from Charles Péguy[42] was, "Everything that begins in mysticism, ends in politics." And the Iona Community seemed to be, in a sense, exemplifying that same spirit and, intriguingly, within a Church of Scotland ethos.'
– *Richard Holloway*

It was a powerful fusion. Being led in worship by George MacLeod had a profound effect on the people who came to Iona, and Ian Mackenzie had plenty of opportunities to observe the impact on worshippers, from his place at the piano:

'I can't speak for other people, but my impression was not that people made resolutions to live a different life, but that they were changed! There was, I would dare to say, a shifting, or movement, of the atoms in their being. They felt transfigured. And among the people who were changed, the ones that I remember with particular vividness were not the members of the Community – because they'd been through a long process of theology, and they knew that this was going to be happening, and it was all part of a career programme – but it was the visitors.'
– *Ian Mackenzie*

From the very beginning, visitors to the island were encouraged to join the Community for worship, and George MacLeod put in place a framework of morning and evening worship which is still discernable in the pattern of worship in the Abbey today:

'The morning service, which was at eight o'clock in order to allow work to begin on the building site, had a set pattern to it, with variations by the day, but with the same basic structure. It was a service taken by craftsmen, as well as by would-be ministers who were joining the Community, or by George MacLeod or Ralph Morton, in turn. The morning service never ended with a benediction, because the benediction came at the end of the evening service, so that the whole day was bracketed by worship. And everybody on Iona became aware, very quickly, that morning service and then evening service held together the daily life of the place.'
– *Douglas Alexander*

'The evening worship was a gathering of a whole lot of other people from the island. Almost every visitor on the island came to the nine o'clock service, and afterwards we stood around and chatted. It was the end of the day, the sun going down. And then we scattered to the various homes on the island.'
– *George Wilkie*

Unlike the morning services, each evening service had its own distinctive character:

'Saturday night was always a service where the worship was one of welcome for those who had just arrived off the steamer earlier in the day. Sunday was traditionally the Quiet Time. It was very simple, almost from the Quaker tradition. But the Quiet Time in the Abbey was an opportunity for so many of us in the Church of Scotland to experience, for the first time in our lives, worship which wasn't crowded out by words, words, words. And many of us found the space that this gave us, something that we treasure, and which we still don't find in the Church of Scotland.

Wednesday would be the Healing Service, with the laying-on of hands, and absolutely nothing spooky, or cheap, or shallow, but in the best New Testament tradition of taking seriously the healing ministry of our Lord. The service had a dignity and a composure about it which was well ahead of its time.

Thursday was the Act of Belief – long before the shenanigans of Billy Graham's evangelical circuses. The Act of Belief Service on Iona provided an opportunity for people, either to make a decision for Christ, or, as was most often the case, to reconfirm one's discipleship. And, again, it was a service of simplicity, and dignity, and composure. And it was uplifting.

And on Friday night, there developed the tradition of a Communion. And that Friday night Communion was deliberately less formal than the traditional Sunday morning observance of the Sacrament.

Sunday mornings were tangibly important. If you were living in the Abbey or the Youth Camps, you knew that Sunday was different. There was just a sense that it was all building up to the 10.30am celebration of the Sacrament which was done with a grandeur – not pomp – pomp would be a thousand miles away from the reality – but done with a grandeur and a dignity which George insisted on, with military precision.

in four-part harmony. What else? That was the thing. And although, at that stage, it was only men in the Community, so you couldn't have sopranos and altos, Reggie was a consummate practitioner at arranging music so it lay in men's voices, and all the golden oldies were sung with a lovely resonance which was beautiful in the Abbey. The Abbey has a wonderful acoustic! So, the 23rd Psalm to "Crimond", and "St George's Edinburgh" every Sunday for the Communion Service. It was a great sound. And then I came along.'
– *Ian Mackenzie*

When, in the mid-1950s, Reggie Barrett-Ayres' already limited sight failed, Ian was recruited as his replacement:

'The brief was clear: play for the services, organise the singing, and rehearse the Youth Camps for the services. That was it. I'd no idea what I was going to do, but that was the brief. It turned out to be a hell of a bloody battle.'
– *Ian Mackenzie*

Ian Renton remembered that time vividly:

'The music was tremendous. It only became ruined once, when Ian Mackenzie took over the music, and he said, "From now on, there will be no harmony sung!" George MacLeod's wife and I led a rebellion against this, and it was bitter.'
– *Ian Renton*

So what lay behind Ian Mackenzie's insistence on unison singing?

'Some of my best friends at New College [Edinburgh University's Divinity Faculty] were post-graduate Europeans – French, German, Swiss – and they produced their own hymnaries from their own countries, and I was absolutely gobsmacked! They were just streets ahead of us.

There was a kind of austere philosophy behind it, but the actual presentation of it was highly practical. For example, there were descants all the way through, not just for voices, but for violin, flute, all the kinds of the things that now you see on *Songs of Praise* all the time –

arrangements for accompanying instrumentalists. They were doing it in the Reformed parts of Europe at the end of the 1930s.

But the austere bit of it was best expressed by Bonhoeffer.[43] He wrote about singing as an act of brotherhood and sisterhood. It was the community in union with each other, and with Christ. And it must be something which formed them together as one body. Therefore, unison, not harmony: not parts, but one line. It focuses the words, but for Bonhoeffer, it was a much deeper thing: it was an acting out of the Gospel in music. This made complete sense to me at that time in my life, when I had just been overwhelmed with the sense of this extraordinary thing that the Gospel really was. And it seemed to me that that was what should be happening on Iona.'

– Ian Mackenzie

What Ian Mackenzie was trying to do was to make George MacLeod's experiment in community incarnate in the music of the Abbey. And while he could see that what Reggie Barrett-Ayres had been doing had played a part in helping the Youth Campers, in particular, to feel that they were part of something bigger – he did not believe that it was appropriate:

'Although the resonance of the Abbey could make it a very beautiful sound, I'd heard some of that kind of singing, and it struck me as "stodgy", and not expressing what the whole Community life was about. It was trying to be something it wasn't. It wasn't a cathedral choir, but it was trying to do that kind of thing. So, I got my two feet on Iona, and I didn't see any point in hanging around. I started to do it all, and that was where the bloodiness came in, because there was an understandable period during which, dismantling the one and simultaneously introducing the other, was difficult. And, often, it didn't work. But there was another element in it which was the emotional element. That was where my naivety, or youthful arrogance, came in. I was just insensitive. I didn't understand how dear all that was. Now I'm an older person, of course, not only do I understand it, but I share exactly what they felt. But it's too late for me to apologise to them now. Not that I repent of what I did. I just think maybe I didn't handle it well.'

– Ian Mackenzie

What followed is clearly still etched in Ian Mackenzie's memory:

'In those days, I was very thin, which, symbolically, can matter. Because Reggie was all nice, and tubby, and friendly, and here I was coming in like a sharp knife, and starting to make them do this. It was a short, sharp shock, and, in the first ten minutes every Saturday evening, I had to do things with them which they thought were insane, and then they actually began to enjoy doing it that way.

But I think where I could have been more tactful is that they naturally thought that the 23rd Psalm and "Crimond" were umbilically linked, and what I did was to say, "Look, I'm not here to introduce lots of flashy new stuff. There is a very great old Scottish tune called 'Martyrs'." And they said, "You can't have 'The Lord's my Shepherd' in a minor key!" People sort of get the verse about "death's dark vale", but this is a happy thing about sheep going "Bah", isn't it? And suddenly here's this grave melody which the Reformers sang. Eventually, by the end of the summer, anybody daring to do "Crimond" would have been laughed out of court, because it suddenly sounded so "ding-dong".'
– *Ian Mackenzie*

But while Ian Mackenzie may have won over the Community and the Youth Campers, he had a still more formidable group of people to persuade:

'What this affected was wives visiting the island, and visitors, and, above all, a phalanx of the "great and good" called "Friends of Iona" who came for two weeks each summer. They weren't members of the Community, but it was a regular ritual, and, for them, the music, and the way it had sounded, was integrated. It was part of the mystique of Iona: dear old Reggie and the gorgeous old hymn tunes sung romantically. And suddenly there was this whippersnapper trying to whippersnap everybody! When I really knew I was in trouble was when I was sitting, playing the piano, and half the congregation had their fingers in their ears. The nice, gentle, old ladies, "Friends of the Community", had their fingers in their ears, as a protest against what I was doing!'
– *Ian Mackenzie*

Faced with the mutiny of the 'Friends of Iona', George MacLeod let his displeasure be known. But later, he took Ian aside:

'He confessed to me at the end of that first three months, "I now understand what you were doing." And he told a lovely story about hearing the rehearsal one night, as he was walking up from the pier. It was becoming a strong gale, and, through the spray, he heard the sound of the rehearsal. And, to him, it was Columba's monks. And, at that point, the penny dropped. He apologised for the fact that he hadn't told me then, but he had his pride, and he wasn't going to collapse that easily.'
– Ian Mackenzie

So despite everything, Ian was invited back the following summer, perhaps because it was not George, but Ralph Morton who was, technically, in charge of the music:

'I'm quite sure Ralph was the instigator of asking me back. He organised everything, including the music. This was a hoot, because Ralph Morton was completely tone-deaf. He couldn't sing. If you heard him singing, it was one long monotone, and he said he had no understanding, or appreciation, of music whatever. But it was his job to look after the music, so, once a week, we would meet to discuss the praise for the following week, and I really loved those sessions, because here was a minister – and this is quite rare – here was a minister in charge of the liturgy, giving, sometimes, a whole morning to a so-called musician – that was me. And he treated me as a musician, not as a theological student, which I then was. Trying to make every bit of praise fit every lesson, and theme. And it turned out he had a very fine grasp of music, in fact. He somehow heard music through his brain. And he was always on my side, because he understood, at once, what I was doing, and the reasons for it. He also was very critical of words. He would say, "We can't have these words!" And this was always based on some theological perspective. He couldn't stand anything to do with the "church militant", or the Kingdom in terms of militancy. And metaphors about the Church as a ship in a storm, he thought, were melodramatic. So we had wonderful

debates – really, really fascinating. They were great tutorials for me, about theology, and about the Community.'
– *Ian Mackenzie*

Ironically, perhaps Ian Mackenzie's greatest contribution to Iona worship was something that didn't fall within the confines of the Service at all:

'I started, almost immediately, to play at the end of the service, an improvised voluntary. The reason I did that was that I was trying to introduce them to new tunes, or tunes which they were not so familiar with, and I used just to do that. And it began to expand, and people began to wait until I'd finished; to listen to them, because they were intrigued. On one occasion, I remember, it lasted half an hour! I couldn't see them, so I wasn't aware if anybody was there or not. And I always tried to tell, in the music, the story of the readings, the lessons, or the sermon. On one occasion, Ralph Morton astounded me. This is the man who was totally tone-deaf. He'd sat listening, and the next morning he told me exactly the story I'd had in mind through it. He decoded it. So that absolutely thrilled me, and, in a way, that was the high point of my musical life, because it had meaning, and people waited.'
– *Ian Mackenzie*

During one of these improvised voluntaries, an American visitor in the congregation became very interested in what Ian was doing:

'This American talked to Ralph. They put their heads together, and they said they thought it was now getting to the stage where the Community on the mainland could do with some creative work on the music of the parishes served by the Community, and would I consider doing that? The deal would be that I would go for a year across to New York, do some studies in New York Union Seminary – there was a Church music college attached to it – and between the seminary in New York and the Community, they would subsidise it. It really was a fantastic offer. And then my job over a period of years would be to try and develop music in Community parishes, and if life had gone that way, I think that would have been very exciting. In fact, John Bell[44] picked up that particular challenge, and I don't regret missing it, because the reasons I gave it up were personal, to do with my mother being ill.

But that was the first step they were taking to develop music as part of their programme. And it's great what John Bell has done, because he's actually evangelised Scotland. His style isn't exactly my style, but he's a serious musician. So, looking at it in terms of providence, maybe I was used for a couple of years to break the mould; to let them see, "There is a problem here. We've got to actually decide what we're going to do in the parishes."'
– Ian Mackenzie

Although Ian Mackenzie then moved north to care for his mother, his work was continued by another young Divinity student, Douglas Galbraith:

'Before I became a "New Man", I was the musician for a summer. I think that must have been one of the most formative experiences I've ever had. There was something about the worship on Iona which allowed people freedom to be more creative than they felt in their home church. A mixture of style and place, but also, I think, a feeling of being, maybe, on the edge of the Church; of being part of something that was a little off-centre. And one responded to that.

Of course, in my case, I had mentors who had done this before: Reginald Barrett-Ayres, Ian Mackenzie, and so on. They had set a pattern of experiment, so there was this feeling of continuing that, if possible. Being asked to play morning and evening, at the beginning and end of worship, immediately said to you, "Now what is relevant to play here? I don't open a book of voluntaries. I don't even open a book." I followed Ian Mackenzie's belief in improvisation, and tended to make new music – of what quality, I've no idea – each time I played.

I also felt it important to interpret words, and felt free to experiment with accompaniments. Now, I have to acknowledge Mackenzie here, because he was a great influence. He showed a lot of us the way here. One of the biggest moments in my life was when Ian came on his

honeymoon to Iona, and I was playing that day, and I improvised something on the first hymn, and on the strength of it, Ian asked me round for supper afterwards. Somehow, the worship on Iona raised questions about the place of music in worship, and I think it's something to do with being at the end of things that gives you more freedom.'
– *Douglas Galbraith*

Certainly, Douglas Galbraith, like Ian Mackenzie before him, used that freedom to experiment with new kinds of Church music. But for Douglas, some of that new music was to come from an unexpected source:

'In my early years as a member of the Community, there were musical opportunities which cemented my link with the Community, and that was when Tom Colvin brought back tapes from Malawi and Ghana. Another Music Master and I decoded those, and we published them as *Free to Serve* and *Leap, My Soul*.'
– *Douglas Galbraith*

Community member Tom Colvin, and his wife, Patsy, lived and worked as missionaries in Malawi and Ghana for a decade. Tom's official responsibility was for education, but his passion was music and worship:

'Tom's two great gifts were in Christian service, and in music and leading worship, and he introduced, wherever possible, the Malawian tunes in worship. He was encouraged to develop that side of worship, and he enjoyed it. It was very, very important to him.

The Iona Community published his first collection of these indigenous tunes – melodies to which he either set new words, or translations of the African language, and it caught on. It struck a chord with quite a lot of groups in the Church. I mean, he used it on deputation, and he used it with the Community. He got people singing some of the very simple ones.

He was also very inspired and guided by the work of a Scottish missionary, Helen Taylor, who, in her own right, had published a small collection, *Tunes from Nyasaland*, in the 1950s. Tom knew, at

once, how very important this was – a seminal work – and he saw her
(she was retired by then), and talked to her about her hymns.

He taped a lot of people singing, and when we were back from
Malawi, when Tom was grieving for Africa, grieving for Malawi, it
was his solace, his comfort, to get all these tapes out, and he just
worked and worked at them. Tom took the tunes down in sol-fa – he
played the piano by ear, largely – but he had the energy, and the determination, and the gift, to write them down, and get people to sing
them, which was the breakthrough.'
– *Patsy Colvin*

Community member and respected hymn-writer Ian Fraser confirms
Patsy's assessment:

'The wide range of hymns, drawing on many nations, and tribes, and
peoples, and the bringing of that into our worship in Scotland, has
been an enrichment to worship.'
– *Ian Fraser*

Free to Serve and *Leap, My Soul* made an enormous impact when they
were first published. It's easy to forget nowadays what ground-breaking
stuff they were:

'These days, it seems entirely right that we should sing African songs
in Iona Abbey! Nowadays, we publish books of world songs, and
think nothing of it. We say we're getting in touch with other churches
and their experience, and they're helping us to praise, but we were
recording and distributing new stuff from Africa in the 1960s.'
– *Douglas Galbraith*

Certainly, most people now assume that the Church's interest in world
music began with 'Wild Goose',[45] but it was, in fact, a product of the early
years of the Community. And people like Tom Colvin and Douglas
Galbraith anticipated 'Wild Goose' in introducing Western Christians to
the riches of African music.

It may also surprise some people to learn that members of the early

Community were writing hymns that reflected the concerns and insights of the Community, decades before Wild Goose existed:

'Iona was very early in the renewal of church music which started in the 1950s and '60s, as was, of course, evidenced in the Dunblane Music Group[46] that Ian Fraser was part of – and I, actually, was part of too. "Wild Goose" were a natural continuation of things that were going on anyway.'
– *Douglas Galbraith*

Ian Fraser was at the very heart of the hymn-writing consultations and workshops of the 1960s, which were based at Scottish Churches' House, Dunblane:

'I would certainly say hymn-writing was a contribution of the Community. That really started in Dunblane, and John Bell and others picked it up. And I would say that the leadership in the relating of worship to people's ordinary daily life, in a fresh way, is mainly a Community contribution. I don't see it coming from Taizé: it was less thirled[47] to the daily working life of people. This comes from the Community. John Bell, and Kathy Galloway, and others have drawn on resources that weren't there before in the hymn books.'
– *Ian Fraser*

Douglas Galbraith picks up this point as being central to an understanding of the Community's relationship to its music:

'I think there's a very strong connection between the social justice concern of the Community and the music that was formed round it, because that's where it came from. I think what happens is that the Church engages in ministry and witness, and it encounters response to that. It's thrown back on itself. And one of the places it turns to is a place which is, at one and the same time, reassuring and envisioning – and that's its music and its hymn-writers.

When you're facing, as a Church, a certain situation, you're at the same time addressing your hymn-writers and saying, "Can you help us here? Can you interpret?" And the hymn-writers respond to that.

And in the very responding to that, they're also saying to the Church, "And here is something else we need you to do." So that the music in the Church is not simply an embellishment of worship, or something which technically allows people to sing together, it's actually an instrument – in another sense – by which the Church takes steps towards renewing its life and its mission.'
– *Douglas Galbraith*

That process, Douglas argues, was particularly apparent in the Community:

'When you think of the actual words that came from the Dunblane Music Group and were earliest heard on Iona – Ian Fraser's "Lord, look upon our working day; busied in factory, office, store" – and you think of the words that Tom Colvin wrote to some of these Malawian and Ghanaian tunes, there's a very strong connection between the social justice concern of the Community, and the music that is formed round it. And, of course, supremely, it's come into its own in the work of the "Wild Goose Group", where the combination of engagement, and prayer, and spirituality is so well-balanced.'
– *Douglas Galbraith*

And Douglas Galbraith believes that the quality of the music produced *by* the Community is a tribute to the robustness and coherence of George MacLeod's original vision *for* the Community:

'Somehow, even though George MacLeod wouldn't consider himself a great musician, Iona attracted the music that matched its own vision. And, that's interesting, because it may say that if you have a vision that's complete enough, or solidly founded, it will attract all it needs, from whatever quarter.'
– *Douglas Galbraith*

And just as that vision has made a significant contribution to the Church worldwide, so too the music and the worship which express that vision have made an enormous impact on the wider church:

'I think that the Community has revolutionised Church of Scotland worship. They moved into a rediscovery of an authentic, vibrant kind of worship that uses theatre, symbol and sacrament. And I think they've influenced not just the Church of Scotland, but all the churches. You will find that the "Iona approach" has influenced worldwide Christianity.'

– *Richard Holloway*

1

2

3

6

7

8

Photos

1. Ralph Morton and George MacLeod were a hard act for young ministers to follow (Faith Aitken archive)

2. The island itself is a 'thin' place (by Aaron Kramer)

3. The building had a humility and a plainness: the west door of the Abbey (Calthorpe Emslie archive)

4. George MacLeod was a master of liturgy (Graeme Brown archive)

5. Ordered worship spoke to young people: Molly Harvey and Tom Buchhan kneeling in the Abbey, 1956 (Molly Harvey archive)

6. Worship in the Abbey was electrifying (Faith Aitken archive)

7. In the Abbey, you look down to the Communion table, not up to an altar (Calthorpe Emslie archive)

8. Craftsmen and ministers sat together in the choir stalls (Iona Community calendar, 1946)

The Community
and Africa

'There's a job coming up in Calabar'

While the Community was, by no means, the only organisation that inspired its members to serve overseas – the Student Christian Movement was also a breeding-ground for missionaries in the 1940s and '50s – nevertheless, a disproportionately large number of Iona Community members and Associates offered themselves as missionaries during those years:

'When the Church history of this time gets written up, the Community will be seen as responsible for encouraging a whole lot of people to work abroad.'
– *Ray Baxter*

In one sense, this is not surprising. In fact, given the Community's emphasis on social justice, and on the commitment of one's whole self to the service of others, linked, it has to be said, with a certain romanticism, it's a wonder that even more 'New Men' did not offer to work on the mission field.

They tended to see themselves as pioneers, rebuilding communities in the most difficult urban parishes, and creating communities from scratch in the new housing schemes to which inner-city dwellers were being decanted. Consequently, those who did not feel that they were cut out to work in such areas of urban deprivation, often felt that they were 'letting the side down', and looked for other ways to stretch themselves, the most obvious of which was foreign mission:

'By the time we got engaged, Bill [Aitken] was working at Fettes College[48] in Edinburgh, but he had already felt it was, in a way, too cushy a job there. He wanted to do something that was more challenging, and he had been persuaded, I think, largely by John Summers, another Community member, to volunteer for what was then called "Foreign Missions". He was to be going to Calabar in Nigeria which was where John Summers had been. I think he persuaded Bill to go out and take his place at the Hope Waddell Training Institution.'
– *Faith Aitken*

Throughout the 1940s and '50s, Calabar, and the Hope Waddell Institute in particular, operated, in effect, as an 'Iona Parish', with one Iona Community man succeeding another.

The Hope Waddell was a secondary school for African boys, which provided both academic education and vocational training. It was education of a very high standard, and some pupils went straight from the Hope Waddell to universities in Britain and the United States. But, because they also offered vocational training, they needed to recruit craftsmen to the teaching staff too, and what better place to find skilled craftsmen than on Iona?

Joe Blair had gone to Iona in 1948 as an apprentice joiner to work on the refectory roof, but after 18 months in the Community, he began to feel that he ought to offer to serve abroad:

'I spoke to Dr MacLeod about it, and he said, "There's a job coming up in Calabar, Nigeria." So I applied to 121 George Street [Headquarters of the Church of Scotland], and I got an interview. In the interval, George MacLeod had written me a reference, and three months after that, I sailed from Liverpool on a banana boat down to the Cameroons, and then we sailed up from Victoria in the "David Livingstone", an old tub, and we arrived at the Calabar River the next day.'
– *Joe Blair*

After initial training, Joe, like Bill Aitken, taught at the Hope Waddell Institute:

'They had motor mechanics. They had printing works. They had marine engineers. They had joiners, and what we called "block-layers". I was involved in the workshops. I dealt with apprentices' training, along with one of the senior missionaries, and when he went home, I took over.'
– *Joe Blair*

Graeme Brown was later to follow the same well-trodden path:

'Between 1961 and 1969 I was based in Nigeria. I found myself doing all kinds of different jobs, but, initially, I was in Calabar Town, in the

first of the secondary schools established in Eastern Nigeria, the Hope Waddell Training Institution, where Bill and Faith Aitken were already on the staff. They were immensely helpful to me when I was settling into Africa, and settling into new work, and settling into chaplaincy.'
– *Graeme Brown*

Like many other Community missionaries, Graeme's initial decision to become a missionary had been profoundly influenced by the example of other Community Men who had already made that choice. Richard Baxter remembers the effect they had on him:

'Tom Colvin rang up to say, "I'm off to Central Africa," and this reminded me that, in college, we had been asked from time to time, "Would you be willing, when you're qualified, to serve overseas?" And I'd always said, "Yes", and I had meant it. But I hadn't remembered that. His going reminded me. So I then went to 121 George Street, Edinburgh, and said, "If I offered, where would you send me?" And they said, "Probably Central Africa." And then we entered into negotiations, and that, in fact, is where I went. Ray and I went to Nyasaland – now Malawi.'
– *Richard Baxter*

It was an exponential process. The more the 'New Men' got to hear of what their fellows were actually doing in Africa, the more compelling the prospect of joining them became:

'There were, at that time, a considerable number of members of the Community in different parts of the world, particularly in Africa. One of my experiences in New College had been to meet Tom Colvin who had been in Central Africa, and I was aware at the time that huge changes were taking place in Central Africa, during the period of the Central African Federation, and Iona Community members had been profoundly involved in trying to resolve that issue.'
– *Graeme Brown*

In short, the experiences of men like Tom Colvin allowed younger members to see the Community's ethos is action, and provided a practical demonstration of one way in which the Community's vision could be enacted on a world stage.

'Are you now, or have you ever been, a member of the
Iona Community?'

Clearly, the inspirational quality of the Community's ethos, the encour-
agement of George MacLeod, and the practical example of members who
were already working in foreign mission was a potent brew. But while the
Community may have been a major driver in getting young people to
offer to work abroad, it didn't necessarily make life very comfortable for
them when they got there.

Richard Baxter found himself under suspicion as an 'Iona Man', despite
the fact that, during his first tour of duty in Nyasaland (now Malawi), he
was not yet a full member of the Community:

'We were sent to Zomba. My job was largely with the Malawians, but
not entirely, because, in Zomba, there were a lot of European civil
servants, so there was a service in English every Sunday. There was
one other minister missionary there, Bob Sawyers, and when the two
of us were there, we took that service alternately.

The first Sunday we were in Zomba, Bob Sawyers preached a political
sermon. Now, Zomba was a place where there was a lot of gossip, and
the word went round that Bob Sawyers had been preaching revolution
to the Africans. He was invited by MI5 to go and talk with them. It
was very polite. They asked him if he had a script of his sermon, and
he said no, he never preached from a script. So they talked a bit about
what he had said and hadn't said, and then they said, "Your new
colleague – is he a member of the Iona Community?" This is MI5
asking about me! They did that, because Tom Colvin was known to
be a member of the Iona Community, and when he had been Leader
of the Scottish Union of Students, they had stayed in the International
Union of Students when it became Communist infiltrated, or influenced. And so Tom was a marked man, and the Community was
marked in that way. And during that four-year tour, I became so fed
up of defending the Community against ridiculous assertions, that
that was one of the reasons why I wrote to George MacLeod, and
asked if I could become a member!'
– *Richard Baxter*

When Bill and Faith Aitken arrived in Nigeria, they also found that their reputation as Iona Community people had preceded them, this time among the missionary fraternity:

> 'It caused some difficulty, I think, because we came out very much labelled as "Iona Community types", and, at the time, there was quite a strong fundamentalist group among the missionaries who were suspicious of the Community. I don't think we realised, in our innocence, but it did become difficult when both Bill and I were saying things that seemed to contradict what boys had been taught in other lessons. You know, things that came up in Religious Education. So it did cause some friction. Personally though, we became very good friends with these other people, and, no doubt, it was very good for us to realise that there were different attitudes, different points of view. Maybe it was good for the boys too to realise there wasn't just one "right" set of attitudes.'
> – *Faith Aitken*

Jim Wilkie was another who found himself interpreting his role as a missionary in ways which were very different from his evangelical colleagues, but very similar to the ways in which Iona Community ministers in poor, urban parishes in Britain interpreted theirs:

> 'I found myself in Zambia, serving a church in their language. That's terribly important, because then you're onto other people's territory. You're never right. They're always right. And you have to learn that, and that is a big lesson. You have to learn that they are the arbiters of what is right and wrong. You don't argue with them; you just say, "Okay", and you try and get absorbed into this.
>
> Now, I found myself in a church which had been founded by Free Church missionaries of the Church of Scotland who were evangelical – who used evangelical language. And so I worked away with this church, and used the language, learned what word meant what, and used it, and preached it as I got better, until I discovered, listening to others at it in their own language, that they used all the language that I translated as evangelical, but they weren't evangelical at all. They were human beings trying to follow the Lord – which is a different

thing! And to do that, they were using the only tools the missionary had given them. And that was an insight that, when it came, just opened up the world as far as understanding what was going on. I had a great time, because they let me into their lives. I was sleeping in their huts, and travelling in their villages, seeing no white people for ten days at a time.'

– *Jim Wilkie*

Though in a very different environment in Calabar, Faith Aitken confirmed that she and Bill also tried to immerse themselves in the lives of the people they had come to serve:

'I think maybe we were more interested in what was going on outside the walls of Hope Waddell than other missionaries were – though it's difficult when you're in a boarding institution. It does tend to take up the whole of your life and your interests. But, for instance, I did some external adult education that was organised from Ibadan University, and used to go out on my bicycle and meet a little group of adult students, and was trying to help them to pass exams. And I valued that getting outside the confines of the institution and meeting other people.

Bill was asked to be in charge of the voting at an election. In Calabar, there was a pretty equal ethnic division between Efiks and Ibos, and, I think, because of this, they asked a foreigner to be in charge. So that was some part of the Iona Community emphasis rubbing off on us – that we wanted to be involved with these other people outside, and wider events that were going on.'

– *Faith Aitken*

And according to Jim Wilkie, there were plenty of other Community missionaries who interpreted their role in that wider 'Iona' context:

'Iona made it easy. What you did was what you had to do, in order to serve these people, and love them. One thing that helped me quite a lot in all of this was a visit I made to Blantyre in Malawi. I went and saw what Lindsay Robertson was doing with forestry. I saw what Richard Baxter was doing in terms of education. These guys were a great inspiration. And so you had role models around the place, and

these were Iona role models that were being offered. So, for example, we had conferences every year during which maybe a couple of hundred people would come and sleep in a village somewhere, and I would go there and train these lay people to lead the congregations in their little villages all the rest of the year. But in order to do that, I had to make sure that there was a water supply, and that meant I had to find out about plumbing, and diesel engines, and all that stuff.'
– *Jim Wilkie*

But sometimes, 'doing what you had to do' was not so easy:

'Then, of course, the whole independence process came along, and the local white District Commissioner came from Isoka, seventy miles away, and said, "We are no longer able to guarantee your safety. You must leave this place, and come and live with us at the Administrative Centre." My colleague Alasdair Morton said, "Well, we'll go and talk to the elders, and see what they advise." So he went, saw the elders, and talked to them, and came back. And the word from them was, "If you think we can't look after you, you better beat it." And so we talked about it, the two families, and agreed to stay. And nobody came near us, because, of course, the people who were causing the trouble were the children of the elders. It was just the next generation of the same crowd. So they put out the word into the villages, "So-and-so's okay. You don't touch him." And that was how it was. We were quite glad we were sleeping under tiles though, and not under thatch, because a lot of the school was under thatch, and it all got burned down round about us. It was quite a time. But, nevertheless, we were okay, and they looked after us.'
– *Jim Wilkie*

However, it would not be in Zambia, but in Nyasaland, that the 'Iona' missionaries' commitment to justice and peace would be supremely tested.

'The perils and dangers of this night'

As Graeme Brown made clear, a number of Iona Community members worked as missionaries in Central Africa during the 1950s and '60s. He mentioned Tom Colvin specifically, but there were others, including

Tom's wife, Patsy; Albert and Jenny McAdam; Kate and Lindsay Robertson; and Richard and Ray Baxter.

It was a time of enormous change, and these Iona Community people were profoundly involved in working for justice and peace in Nyasaland. The key issue of the time was the desire of the people of the region for self-determination and, ultimately, independence.

When Richard and Ray Baxter were first posted there, Nyasaland was being governed as part of the Central African Federation. They arrived in Zomba in 1954, shortly after the imposition of the hated Federation:

'In 1953, the Federation of Nyasaland and the Rhodesias had been imposed. And it was imposed against the wishes of the people in Nyasaland. Because, although there were perhaps good rational reasons for making a Federation where Nyasaland provided the labour, Southern Rhodesia provided the know-how, and Northern Rhodesia provided the resources, the people in Nyasaland knew – because so many of the men went away and worked in Rhodesia or South Africa – that Southern Rhodesia would be the dominant partner, and that their race attitude was a very hard one, like South Africa's. It wasn't embodied in law at that time, but the post offices had different entrances, or they had an entrance for the Europeans, and a window at which the Africans could stand. It was a definite two-tier thing. They knew that, and they were hoping for their own political advancement in Nyasaland, and they knew that that would be stopped. And they were quite right. The Federation happened, and some of the departments were federalised right away. One of them was the Medical Department, and the first action after the Federal folk took over was to remove the sheets from the African hospital, because, in Rhodesia, Africans didn't have sheets. That's an absolute concrete illustration of the attitude.'
– *Richard Baxter*

Nevertheless, there had been a kind of logic behind the creation of the Federation, as Patsy Colvin points out:

'It was politically sensible, or so they thought, to focus the administration of the three territories in Salisbury, in the hands of the whites, because neither Nyasaland nor Northern Rhodesia had progressed very far in terms of colonial development. They still had Councils, Protectorate Legislative Councils, where the African people were represented, but the government of the Protectorate was in the hands of white administrators – Governors.

When I went out, I could see that that was becoming more and more an issue for everybody – not just for the people of Nyasaland, but for the people in the Colonial Office in London. And the churches' interest was also sharpened and deepened, because the injustice of the situation was obvious. And because the Church in Scotland has these long links – very important and very lively links – with that part of Africa, it wasn't difficult to grab their attention.'
– *Patsy Colvin*

Patsy and Tom Colvin arrived in Nyasaland at a critical moment then. A critical moment not only for the State, but for the Church:

'The Church of Central Africa Presbyterian was a partner with the Foreign Mission Committee in Edinburgh. Everything was done by a Mission Council with African representatives on it, but every department – education, building, health, hospital, printing – were all headed up by expatriate missionaries from the Church in Edinburgh. And that was under examination.

The Mission Council was, in many ways, restrictive, and it was, for us younger people, oppressive. There were lots and lots of young, able African teachers, medical assistants, printers, builders, ministers. More and more were being trained who were very capable of taking decisions for the Church. And in the best traditions of the founders – the founders of the Mission who came from Scotland in the 1870s – visionary men and visionary women – a Joint Council developed with the Malawians.'
– *Patsy Colvin*

Patsy's husband, Tom, used his position as a Mission Partner to facilitate this process of 'Africanisation':

'Tom Colvin, in his job of Education Secretary, was enabling Africans to take more responsibility. For example, I was Manager of Schools, but my successor was Desmond Kwayera, who was the Headmaster of the primary school.'
– *Richard Baxter*

But these moves towards 'Africanisation' in Church and Mission were not being mirrored politically, and men like Tom Colvin felt compelled to use what influence they had, to support the independence movement in Nyasaland:

'Tom and our friends preached every now and then. If it was an English service, there would be severe criticism after the sermon. In one or two cases, a white administrator walked out of church, and the secret police – well, they were the Federal Police – did send somebody to church to listen to what was said.

In those first years, Tom and I had a group of young graduate Malawians – Africans – meeting regularly for discussion and study. They came to our house, and some of our senior colleagues were not very happy about this, because some of these young people had been educated in Uganda, and they knew about the African National Congress, and how it was doing, and the forward movements for African independence.

Being in Blantyre, we were in touch with people who were thinking, and older people, as well as the young lions who had come back from overseas degrees and training. Dr Banda, who was their leader, came back in 1958, and met a lot of people in our house. African leaders from the various departments of the Mission came and greeted him in our house.'
– *Patsy Colvin*

'Dr Banda was the most educated Malawian in the world. He had been a doctor in Edinburgh, he'd been a doctor in London, and he'd then gone out to Ghana, but he had said he would not go back to Nyasaland until it was free.

The young men who were the Nyasaland National Congress, however, needed a solid figure at the top, and they begged him to come back and be that figure, and he did. And he was going up and down the land, saying that his object was to break this stupid Federation, and bring self-government and independence to Nyasaland. And so, things were getting more and more tense.

I came home on leave in February 1959, and I was on the ship coming home, when the Emergency was declared, and all the educated Africans were detained. And so when I got home, I was the man straight from the Field, and I went on television, having hardly ever seen it even.

I was a very unpolitical chap in many ways. I wasn't personally involved to the extent that Tom Colvin, and Andrew Ross, and Albert McAdam were, but nevertheless, when I came home that time, I had become politicised. I wrote a letter to a lot of our friends talking about the situation, and how I read it, and the fact that I was writing this while I was at home, because I was not at all sure that correspondence would not be read by the authorities in Nyasaland. I said that the Nyasaland Africans did not want the Federation.'
– *Richard Baxter*

Other 'Iona missionaries' also tried to influence the Church and the government back in Britain:

'We brought back the truth that the people of Malawi were under this oppressive yoke of a hated Federation, and wanted to be free of it. We knew when we were going on leave in 1958 that the crunch was coming. That it would have to be hard times ahead. And, of course, we were back in Scotland for the 1959 General Assembly when there were motions in support of the Nyasaland determination to seek independence. There were some very strong voices in the Church opposed to Nyasaland's freedom. There were right-wing people who had been High Commissioners, and had been involved with the politics of it. And in that crucial Assembly debate, there were very strong voices and counter-motions to the one that said the Church of Scotland is behind independence and is behind freedom for the people of Nyasaland.'
– *Patsy Colvin*

In that General Assembly of 1959, however, George MacLeod's voice was strongest:

'The Church of Scotland had its Special Committee on Central Africa, of which George MacLeod was the Convener, and because of that, the Assembly made good decisions and representations to the government.'
– *Richard Baxter*

Unfortunately, the British government chose to ignore these representations, and, for one Iona missionary couple, the personal consequences of speaking out against the Federation were devastating:

'The movement to free Nyasaland from the Federation had gathered a huge amount of support in Scotland, and after the General Assembly of 1959, the Federal authorities came up from London specially to serve Tom with a P.I. – a Prohibited Immigrant Notice, by hand.

We were in the Church of Scotland furlough house in Milngavie. I remember it was the morning, and this car drew up outside the door. I was at the back of the house, hanging out washing, and I looked round, and saw this big car, and a driver, and a man in a suit. I went in, and Tom had read what was in the letter, and then it was just a feeling of shock. There was no way of appealing against these notices. Protest, yes. But that was the final word, because they were a properly constituted part of the British Commonwealth, and this was from Salisbury. If they said, "We're suspending you", there was no use getting on a plane. We'd be turned around and sent back. That was it. We were P.I.'d!

It was devastating for Tom, because that was June, and we were due to go back in August. We'd left a lot behind – a lot of work that Tom wanted to get on with. And then it was just a feeling of anticlimax, I suppose, because the Assembly had been a high point. You had felt you were onto something that was inevitable, that was going to happen, though it would take time. And, of course, we were young, and the question was, "Well, what next?" But it was really dealing with the shock, and the awful drop. We couldn't really think of what came next.'
– *Patsy Colvin*

But if the Colvins were devastated to find themselves prohibited from returning to Nyasaland, their Iona colleagues who remained in the country had to face an even more devastating choice – whether to stay or go, when the Emergency was declared:

'Andrew Ross, and Fergus McPherson who was up in the north and who was the Principal of Livingstonia [Mission Station] at the time, were given the offer of being removed from the situation into safety. Fergus called together the Senatus of Livingstonia which included the missionaries, and the African minister, and one or two others, and they discussed it very carefully. Things were happening. People were getting hurt, because in the north, in particular, they regarded this as a declaration of war by the government. And, of course, they sent up young Southern Rhodesian recruits who behaved abominably, and people were shot. People were killed. And Europeans were afraid, because what the Governor said was that he had found a plot that all Europeans were to be killed. So Fergus put this before the missionaries. They were being offered the chance to withdraw. There was going to be a boat on the lake [Lake Nyasa] that would take them away. So they discussed it, and they decided that they would stay. And the African minister said, "May I say something?" And Fergus said, "Oh yes." And he said, "If you had decided to go, we would have understood, but it would have broken the Body of Christ."

Some of them, of course, were very much afraid, and had a right to be.'
– *Richard Baxter*

But not only did the missionaries face physical threats from the Southern Rhodesian recruits who were running riot across Northern Nyasaland, they found themselves isolated from, and abandoned by, the white, European population who could not understand their decision to stay:

'In Mulanje, where Hamish Hepburn was, all the other missionary members of staff were women. His wife was there, the doctor was a woman, the women's worker was a woman, the nursing sisters were women. The army came to offer them sanctuary, and they said, "No thank you. Who are we being saved from? The people round about us with whom we work?"

There was tremendous resentment against Hamish and the Mission in general, and the little service in English that was held once a month up in the Planters' Church dwindled to practically nobody coming.'
– *Richard Baxter*

Finally, the situation was resolved by the release from detention of Dr Banda:

'It resolved itself when Ian McLeod became the Colonial Secretary, and his attitude was quite different. He saw that it was the leaders [of the Nyasaland National Congress] that had been taken away and put in detention. They had had a great educational time together, thinking about the future of Nyasaland, while in detention. And so Dr Banda was released.'
– *Richard Baxter*

Following the release of Banda, there was an initial period of great optimism and hope for the future of an independent Malawi, and the Iona missionaries found themselves, unexpectedly, at the heart of things:

'Andrew Ross, Albert McAdam and others had used to go and visit the detainees regularly when they were in prison. And when there was self-government, and then independence, these relationships remained, and the people with whom they had had the relationships became ministers of the government.'
– *Richard Baxter*

The euphoria, however, did not last long:

'Six months after independence, six of the ministers challenged Dr Banda over the issue of whether it was going to be one-man government or cabinet government. Banda had been made up to "Doctor knows best", and really made up to a figure beyond human.

He was making decisions without reference to the Ministers of the Departments, and they would learn about these decisions, simply because of the European secretaries who were there. This was an impossible situation, so they challenged him, and he then held a special meeting of the Legislative Council, and made it a Motion of Confidence.

Now, all of these ministers voted for him – they weren't trying to oust him. There was a tremendous stir at that point. The ministers who had done the challenging called a meeting of their constituents in Limbe, in order to explain to them why they had raised the question, and Banda issued an order that made that meeting illegal. He said that any public meeting had to have five days' prior notice from the police that it was okay, and there wasn't enough time. So it was going to be illegal, if it happened. But once you'd passed the word that there was going to be a meeting, there was no way of stopping the meeting, and so it happened. It happened on a Sunday. Thugs had been brought up from the Lower River – Malawi Young Pioneers – in order to break it up. There was violence. There were people injured, and there were people killed.'
– *Richard Baxter*

On that fateful Sunday, Richard and his wife, Ray, were at home, as Richard had been due to preach that evening:

'I was minister, at that time, of St Michael's and All Angels at Blantyre, and we had an arrangement with the Anglicans that we had the evening service alternately. It was going to be in the Anglican church, and it was my turn to preach. So on the Sunday afternoon, I sat down to prepare my sermon, and I got a phone call from Willie Chokani, who had been the Headmaster in the Hope Waddell Institute and was now a minister of the government, saying, "Richard, go now to Chichiri, collect Grace, Willie's wife, and Augustine Bwanausi's wife, and take them to the Mission for safety. There's been trouble here. Don't wait. Do it now." So I got the Land Rover, and I went. I arrived to find the wives, and their families, who knew nothing about this, of course. They knew their husbands had gone to a meeting, and that was it.

After a while, Willie Chokani and Augustine Bwanausi arrived back, and they went away and were closeted with their wives. When they emerged, they had decided that Willie, and Augustine Bwanausi and

his wife would all skip the country, and that only Grace Chokani would come back to the Mission. Meantime, Ray and Jenny McAdam had sorted out that we would have the Bwanausis, and she would have the Chokanis, so Grace went to the McAdams. And later, this was one of the things that was held against Albert McAdam by the supporters of Banda.'
– *Richard Baxter*

From that day on, Albert McAdam was a marked man. His decision, along with that of other Iona missionaries, to remain loyal to the men they had encouraged during the years of the Federation, comforted during their time in detention, and rejoiced with when they were appointed ministers in Banda's government, had sealed Albert's fate. The fact that these men were now 'personae non gratae' with the Banda government meant that Albert too was unwelcome in Banda's Malawi:

'There was violence of all kinds. People were being picked up in the river with their hands tied. One of Albert's friends had his house fire-bombed, and came to Albert, asking for help to store such furniture as he'd managed to save. And Albert gave that help, because they didn't suddenly cease to be friends just because the government didn't like them. And that was another thing that was held against him. And so, for a while there was a death threat out for Albert, and there were soldiers – police – appointed to guard the house every night. And then the Police Chief came to me and said, "There is a serious death threat. We are not able to protect the McAdams. Please tell them to go." I said, "I've no authority to tell them to go. I'll tell them what you said." And I did. Albert and Jenny said, "We were invited here by the Church of Central Africa Presbyterian. If they tell us to go, we'll go, but not otherwise." And so the General Secretary and others had to think very carefully, and asked them, for their own safety, to go. And then the police came, and said, "Now that it's known that they're going in a week's time, it's all right." And they left.'
– *Richard Baxter*

Those like Richard and Ray Baxter who were left behind, now entered a period of great difficulty:

'That was a time when the country was absolutely split, and the congregations were split. I was preaching Sunday by Sunday, and I would have to find sermons that didn't have any possible political overtones. I was looking through old sermons and I was astonished to find how many of them, without any sort of conscious thing, could be seen as being specifically political.'
– *Richard Baxter*

'What Richard didn't tell you was that he actually got into trouble with Dr Banda, and was called in to explain why we were running courses about marriage. And after that, Richard really just didn't feel he could do anything, because he was always looking over his shoulder. And that's certainly the thing I remember about that time – that you were very careful about what you said to anybody. And my memory of coming home eventually at the end of 1969 was that, at least you could talk, and that was good. But it showed you some of the pressures that, perhaps, we accepted, but it wasn't comfortable.'
– *Ray Baxter*

The adjective which both Ray and Richard repeatedly use to describe the rest of their time in Malawi is 'uncomfortable', but it's clear that the term which most accurately describes their situation is 'dangerous':

'I think the most uncomfortable time was our last few years, because we were quite near Chipembere[49] country at that point. That's where the Lay Training Centre was. And, in fact, a lot of the Anglican people of whom we'd become partners were Chipembere supporters. And one of the things we all did, all the European staff, was that we left our keys in our cars, so that if people needed to get away, they could do so. Nowadays, I wonder if I would do it, but, in those days, we did.

We have a memory – the family, as a whole, has a memory – a very uncomfortable memory of going on holiday. This was after the cabinet crisis, after Banda had taken over totally, but there were still a lot of thugs who would just have roadblocks. And I remember going up to the lake on holiday, and we were stopped at a roadblock, and asked for our Malawi Congress cards. Well, Europeans weren't supposed to have them, so you knew there was something fishy, and Richard just

turned the car and moved away. I think there was a bus as well, so that he was able to do it very easily. And we went to the next place, and went to the police, and got a police escort. And, certainly, our children all remember that journey as being pretty uncomfortable. I think I at least pretended to be very calm, because the children were all there, but it wasn't comfortable.'
– *Ray Baxter*

'And there was a time when we were helping to pack up for people who were having to go, and our daughter, Julie, who was the oldest, said, "When is it our turn to go?" There was no question that they felt the tension there. I often think that that was the time when I really learned to say, "Lighten our darkness we beseech thee, O Lord, and, by thy great mercy, defend us from the perils and dangers of this night" – with a real sense of the perils and dangers.'
– *Richard Baxter*

In short, Richard and Ray were part of a generation of Iona missionaries who risked their very lives in order to honour that commitment to justice and peace which was central to their understanding of the Gospel and of their membership of the Community.

But, not surprisingly, in this African crucible, the untainted idealism of the Community Plenary Session regularly ran full tilt into the messy practicalities of realpolitik. It was an experience that led more often to moral ambiguity than moral certitude.

'If you're going to have peace, you've got to have justice'

Anyone who has worked as a missionary in a culture very different from his or her own will testify that it forced him to make difficult choices, or caused her to reassess many of the certainties with which she set out.

None of the Iona missionaries describes this process better than Graeme Brown. Like all the other Africa-based missionaries, he had to learn to live with ambiguity:

'One of my responsibilities was to be Chaplain of Calabar Prison in

Nigeria. Bill Aitken had been Chaplain there, and he brought me down and introduced me to the prison staff and to the prisoners. It was actually a convict prison where executions took place, and Bill had quite steadfastly refused to have anything to do with these public executions. And I followed him in that, initially. But then some staff from the prison took me aside, and said, "These men are going to their deaths without the support and help of a Chaplain, and you may keep a clear conscience about this, but what about them?" So I re-thought this matter, and I decided that I would take a particular interest in those who were in the condemned cells, visit them regularly, and attend them before, and at, their execution.

It was one of the most awful experiences of my ministry. But I did realise how important that ministry was, because, by getting to know of the cases of these prisoners, I was able to re-open the cases where I thought that justice had not been done, and, in one particular case, there was a reprieve, and I was very grateful for that. Then, the civil war came, and issues of war and peace, and of violence and non-violence became very acute.

I was in the Biafran enclave during the civil war. My worst experience during that time was when I went, for a period of four months, to take charge of food distribution from the one remaining airport that was operating. In all, during that period from 1967 to 1970, there were five thousand sorties of aircraft into Biafra, and something like sixty-three thousand tons of food and drugs were flown in. I was at the airport when the Biafran army returned, and they were hungry like everyone else, so they would hold up the lorries at gunpoint, and steal the food.

I was actually still a pacifist, but I eventually decided the only responsible thing to do, if that food was to get through to the people in the Feeding Centres – those who needed it most – was actually to arm the lorries. The following day, I went out and I saw the bodies of those who'd been shot along the roadside, and that was a terrible experience.

I'd had to face up to the question of the conditions under which it was sometimes necessary to use force. I had to think through what I

Of course, in that respect, Iona missionaries were no different from other returning missionaries: they felt out of place and uncomfortable in Britain. But, for them, there was the safety net of the Community. There, they felt at home. The interest, acceptance and affirmation which had supported them throughout their years abroad continued when they returned to Britain. The precious fruits of genuine community withstood the tests of both time and distance, and are a testament to the quality of the relationships that were originally forged on Iona.

1

2

3

6

7

Photos

1. Joe Blair (front row, 5th left) with pupils of the Hope Waddell Institution, Calabar, Nigeria, 1953 (Joe Blair archive)

2. John Summers (left) and Joe Blair (right) at the christening of their respective children in Nigeria (Joe Blair archive)

3. Richard Baxter (4th from left) with members of Zomba Presbytery, Malawi (Richard Baxter archive)

4. Jim Wilkie dedicates a new village church, Zambia (Jim Wilkie archive)

5. Tom Colvin with Willie Chokani (left), Malawi, 1958 (Patsy Colvin archive)

6. 'Iona men' worked towards the Africanisation of Church and Mission: staff of the Henry Henderson Primary School, Blantyre Mission, Malawi, 1957 (Patsy Colvin archive)

7. Worship in the chapel at Chilema, Malawi (Richard Baxter archive)

8. Children from Uli gather round a Relief plane which crashed, Biafra, 1969 (Graeme Brown archive)

9. Joe Blair's isolated home in Abakaliki, Nigeria (Joe Blair archive)

10. George MacLeod's visit to Malawi: his support was crucial to the 'Iona missionaries' (Richard Baxter archive)

CND and set up the 'Committee of 100'. This was a more militant organisation which advocated civil disobedience rather than the demonstration march, as the appropriate method of protest against weapons of mass destruction.

42. Charles Péguy (b.1873) was a Christian and a socialist. He was prepared to criticise any institution, including the Church, if he felt that it had failed to live up to the demands of truth and justice.

43. Dietrich Bonhoeffer was a German theologian who, when Hitler came to power in 1933, became a spokesman for the Confessing Church, the focus of Protestant resistance to the Nazis. He set up the underground seminary of the Confessing Church, and his book *Life Together* describes the life of the Christian community in that seminary. He was arrested for his part in a plot to assassinate Hitler, and hanged in April 1945.

44. John Bell is a minister of the Church of Scotland and a member of the Iona Community. He is employed full time in the areas of music and worship with the Wild Goose Resource Group. John has produced many collections of original hymns and songs (some in collaboration with Graham Maule), and two collections of songs of the World Church. He lectures in theological colleges in Britain and the USA, but is primarily concerned with the renewal of congregational worship at grassroots level.

45. The Wild Goose Resource Group is a semi-autonomous project of the Iona Community. It exists to enable and equip congregations and clergy in the shaping and creation of new forms of relevant, participative worship.

46. In 1962, a working party was set up, representing a number of denominations, and based at Scottish Churches' House, Dunblane. It was convened by Reggie Barrett-Ayres, and met under the guidance of Ian Fraser who was, at that time, Warden of Scottish Churches' House. Its main aim was to explore recent developments in church music, and it produced two collections of new hymns and songs entitled *Dunblane Praises*.

47. Thirled is a Scots word meaning 'bound' or 'tied'.

48. Fettes College is a well-known Edinburgh public school, founded in 1870. Old Fettesians include one British Prime Minister, three Chancellors of the Exchequer and three Leaders of the Iona Community.

49. It was Henry Chipembere who had planned the meeting in Blantyre which was banned by Dr Banda, ostensibly because he had not obtained police permission. Subsequently, Chipembere attempted a coup d'état. He was defeated, and spent the rest of his life in exile.

50. *Coracle* is the magazine of the Iona Community.

Maps

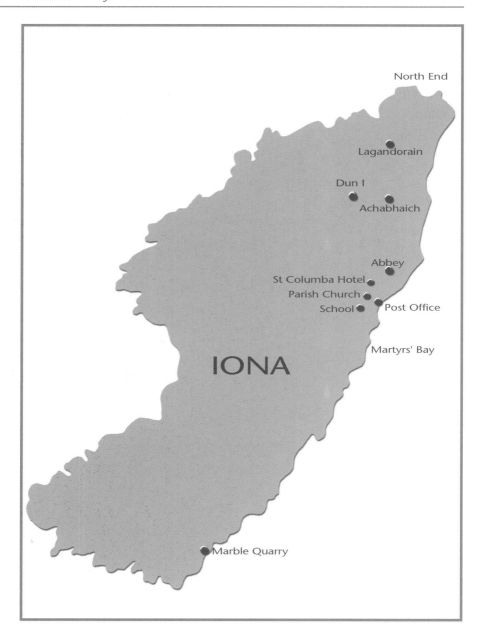

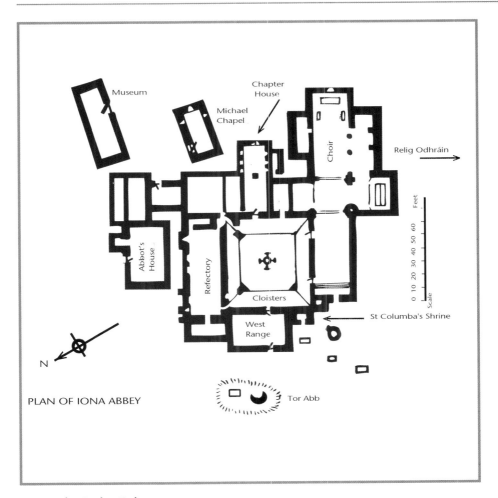

Drawing by Gordon Hicks

A final word?

This, of course, is not the end of the story. The Iona Community continues to develop, in response to the changing needs of our world.

Nor is it the whole story of the Early Years. There will, inevitably, be voices and perspectives which have been missed.

If you have a story about the Early Years of the Community (1938-1969) which you would like to add to those of the interviewees, I would be glad to hear it.

You can e-mail your story to me at: *oralhistory@iona.org.uk* or through our blog page at *www.ionabooks.com/blog/oralhistory* which has been set up so that people can share further stories and photos of the early days of the Community.

Alternatively, you can mail it to me at:

Anne Muir
Oral History Project
The Iona Community
4th Floor, Savoy House,
140 Sauchiehall Street,
Glasgow, Scotland, UK
G2 3DH

www.ionabooks.com/blog/oralhistory

Also from Wild Goose Publications
www.ionabooks.com

George MacLeod
Founder of the Iona Community
Ron Ferguson

The definitive biography of one of the twentieth century's most fascinating and influential churchmen, an outspoken challenger to the status quo and the founder of the radical and often controversial Iona Community.

ISBN 978-1-901557-53-4

Chasing the Wild Goose
The story of the Iona Community
Ron Ferguson

The history of the Iona Community including St Columba's founding of an influential Celtic Christian community on the Hebridean island of Iona in the sixth century; the work of George MacLeod whose inspiration placed Iona firmly on the Christian map once again in the twentieth century; and the current broad span of the Community with its concerns for spirituality, politics, peace and justice.

ISBN 978-1-901557-00-8

Iona: God's Energy
The vision and spirituality of the Iona Community
Norman Shanks

What is it that interests so many people in the work of the Iona Community and draws thousands of visitors each year to the tiny island of Iona? A book about the spirituality, concerns and activities of the Iona Community.

ISBN 978-1-905010-58-5

Wild Goose Publications, the publishing house of the Iona Community established in the Celtic Christian tradition of Saint Columba, produces books, e-books, CDs and digital downloads on:

- holistic spirituality
- social justice
- political and peace issues
- healing
- innovative approaches to worship
- song in worship, including the work of the Wild Goose Resource Group
- material for meditation and reflection

For more information:

Wild Goose Publications
Fourth Floor, Savoy House
140 Sauchiehall Street,
Glasgow G2 3DH, UK

Tel. +44 (0)141 332 6292
Fax +44 (0)141 332 1090
e-mail: admin@ionabooks.com

or visit our website at
www.ionabooks.com
for details of all our products and online sales